M000306027

Not-So-Desperate

Not-So-Desperate

fantasy, fact, and faith on Wisteria Lane

Shawnthea Monroe

CHALICE
PRESS
ST. LOUIS, MISSOURI

© Copyright 2006 by Shawnthea Monroe

All rights reserved. For permission to reuse content, please contact Copyright Clearance Center, 222 Rosewood Drive, Danvers, MA 01923, (978) 750-8400, www.thenewcopyright.com.

Bible quotations, unless otherwise noted, are from the *New Revised Standard Version Bible,* copyright 1989, Division of Christian Education of the National Council of the Churches of Christ in the United States of America. Used by permission. All rights reserved.

Cover art: © Getty Images, Inc.
Photo of author on back cover by Gabriel Haney from Haney's Photography in
        Moorhead, Minnesota. Copyright © 2006 Haney's Photography.
Cover and interior design: Elizabeth Wright

Visit Chalice Press on the World Wide Web at
www.chalicepress.com

10 9 8 7 6 5 4 3 2 1   06 07 08 09 10

Library of Congress Cataloging–in–Publication Data

Monroe, Shawnthea.
   Not-so-desperate : fantasy, fact, and faith on Wisteria Lane / Shawnthea
Monroe.
      p. cm.
   Includes bibliographical references.
   ISBN-13: 978-0-827225-13-8 (pbk. : alk. paper)
   ISBN-10: 0-827225-13-X (pbk. : alk. paper)
   1. Desperate housewives. 2. Television broadcasting—Religious aspects. I.
Title.
   PN1992.77.D49M66 2006
   791.45'72—dc22
                                                            2006006280
          Printed in the United States of America

This book is dedicated to Neil Mueller, the love of my life, and the three greatest blessings I will ever know: Walter, Clara and Ren.

Contents

Acknowledgments

Throughout this journey down Wisteria Lane, I've been surrounded by a great cloud of witnesses to whom I am indebted. I offer my deepest thanks:

To Rose Mary Dougherty, who brought me a word from the Lord, and Pablo Jiménez, who brought me a word from Chalice Press;

To Shannon Craigo-Snell, Andrea Walker, and Tom Long, for their abiding friendship, keen theological insights, and inspiring faith;

To my dear friends who make my life rich indeed: Jane Millikan, Rooth Varland, Nell Devane, Verity Jones, Lillian Daniel, Miriam Jorgensen, Kaia Monroe, Cherie Parker, Nancy Spooner-Mueller, Wendy Miller, Pat Nelson, Angelique Kube, and Margaret Crockett-Dickerman;

To the not-so-desperate women who let me tell their stories: Bonita, Zella, Jennifer, Carol, Christine, Mary, Madeline, Lydia, Marla, Marilyn, Peggy, and a host of others who wish to remain nameless;

To Keith Tandy, who managed to teach me how to subordinate clauses;

And to the wonderful people of the First Congregational United Church of Christ in Moorhead, Minnesota, for blessings too numerous to name.

Last, thanks to the cast and crew of *Desperate Housewives,* without whom this book would not be possible—or necessary.

Introduction

A year or so ago I would not have guessed that I would write a book about *Desperate Housewives*. Sure, I'd heard of Susan and the gals of Wisteria Lane. During that first season, you could hardly open a magazine or turn on the television without hearing about ABC's runaway hit *Desperate Housewives*. But I stayed away. Who wants to see another show about the problems of impossibly thin women with money? It sounded like *Sex and the City* with a carpool.

Then an editor called and asked if I would consider reflecting on and reacting to *Desperate Housewives* from a Christian point of view. Reluctantly, I agreed to take a look. Ten minutes into the pilot episode—after Mary Alice's suicide but before Gabrielle had sex with her teenage gardener on the dining room table—I thought, "This is insane! There's nothing here to reflect on! It's complete trash!" But I kept watching.

Who was I supposed to identify with? Clueless Susan or bloodless Bree? Exhausted Lynette or sexpot Gabrielle? Everything on Wisteria Lane is exaggerated, from the houses to the housewives. Yet hidden within the lush landscape are the mundane issues of real life: marriage, parenting, intimacy, friendship, careers, even faith. Maybe there was something here after all.

I may not have been a fan of *Desperate Housewives* when I started, but I've always been a fan of popular culture, especially as a source of Christian insight and inspiration. (If you're teaching a confirmation course on evil, I know just the right episode of *The X-Files* to use.) I believe what Paul wrote, "All things work for good together for those who love God" (Rom. 8:28), even *Desperate Housewives*. So I agreed to write a book.

Let me be clear. This is not "The Gospel According to *Desperate Housewives*"—though I think "The Gospel According to Bree" might make a great seminary ethics class. This is not a liberal Christian defense of *Desperate Housewives*. The show has nothing to apologize for—it aims no higher than campy entertainment, and it squarely hits the mark. And this is not a sharply worded and brilliantly researched feminist critique of Susan and the gang. I leave that to scholars who are smarter and angrier than I.

Instead, this book is an extended and sometimes cheeky Christian meditation on one of the most popular shows on television. Using the characters and plot lines as a starting point, I explore how real women meet the everyday challenges and temptations of modern life. If we pay attention, there is much to be learned. So whether you are a long-time fan of the show or a curious neophyte, join me as we stroll through the manicured lawns and tawdry plots of *Desperate Housewives* looking for some signs of Jesus' good news, and discover why we are not so desperate.

CHAPTER 1

Who Do You Say That I Am?

At a regional conference on women in ministry in Boston, Massachusetts, I made a public announcement: "I'm doing research for a book about *Desperate Housewives*. If you watch the show, I'd love to talk with you." Given the reaction of the crowd, you would have thought I'd asked "How many of you intend to steal the towels from the hotel this weekend?" The silence was deafening.

But as I was standing at a buffet table that evening, a woman slipped into line by me and asked in a conspiratorial tone, "Are you the *Desperate Housewives* woman?" Answering her out of the corner of my mouth, I whispered, "Yes. Do you watch it?" She glanced around to make sure no one was listening. "I wouldn't miss it. Follow me." We made our way to a secluded table where she confessed her sin—she was a fan. Turns out she isn't alone.

When *Desperate Housewives* debuted in the fall of 2004, it took the television world by storm. The first Nielsen ratings placed it as ABC's biggest series start since 1995.[1] It seems that American television viewers were sick of reality TV, the ranting of Simon Cowell, and *Survivor* retreads. (Doesn't it seem strange that they keep pitting people against the challenges of tropical climates? Isn't it time for something really challenging, like *Survivor: Fargo,* in which twenty-four contestants are stranded at the crossroads of I-94 and I-29 in mid-January? Forget weaving fishing nets out of bamboo. Let's see someone make jumper cables from chicken wire and clothespins. Of course the wind chill would pose a problem for those festive tikki torches during the tribal council meetings, but it's worth a try.) The cry from TV viewers was loud and clear: "Less reality! More tank tops!"

In the fall of 2004 21.3 million people were watching the antics of Susan and the gang. By the end of the 2004–2005 season, *Desperate Housewives* was the fourth most popular show on prime time, pulling in approximately 23 million viewers every Sunday night.[2] At the end of 2005, *Desperate Housewives* was pulling in 25.5 million viewers.[3] In January of 2006, *Desperate Housewives* won the Golden Globe award for most popular television comedy/drama.

Given that no one I knew would cop to watching the show, I wondered, who *are* these viewers? It turns out that the audience is just as attractive as the stars, from an advertiser's point of view. *Desperate Housewives* is a hot commodity among the coveted 18–49 demographic, the movers and shakers of our consumer culture.[4] Among the upscale demographic—defined as people between the ages of 25–54 with household incomes over $100,000—Desperate Housewives is the highest rated show.[5] (Oddly enough, these are the *same* target demographics for most tall-steeple pastors!)

Another startling discovery came from Maria Elena Fernández, who writes for the *Los Angeles Times.* "Those *Desperate Housewives* sure have a lot to hide, but here's one dirty little secret that has caught the television industry by surprise: Nearly 40 percent of the show's viewers are men."[6] According to Fernández, only *Monday Night Football, CSI,* and *The Simpsons* are more popular with the XY group. When I mentioned this surprising discovery to my husband, he said, "I wonder how many of them watch it with the sound off?" Another male friend, who admitted to watching *Desperate Housewives* "because my wife likes it," said, "desperate women in hot pants—what's not to like?"

Of course not everyone likes *Desperate Housewives*. A number of conservative critics have railed against the titillating and tawdry exploits of the ladies of Wisteria Lane. The conservative Parents Television Council listed it among the worst shows for family viewing for 2005.[7] And yet *Desperate Housewives* is consistently ranked as one of the most popular shows in such button-down red-state markets as suburban Atlanta and Salt Lake City. It would seem that some people don't wait until Monday to forget what the pastor said.

Desperate Housewives has become a worldwide phenomenon. As I write, the show is making its debut in China, where, in a brilliant bit of translation, it's called *Crazy Housewives*. It also runs about five minutes shorter than it does on American TV because of a bit of government editing.

There is no doubt about it. The show is a monster hit, even if few of my friends are tuning in. And like all big cultural phenomena, it's working its way into our public vocabulary and collective consciousness. Dry cleaning bags serve as billboards, reassuring us that "Everyone has a little dirty laundry." T-shirts emblazoned with the words "I Know What You Did" are appearing at the mall. And I recently heard a preteen girl evaluate her friend's clothing choice with the words, "That's sort of 'Bree.'" (I assumed she meant uptight and conservative, not vengeful and murderous.)

I've always liked to keep up with modern culture, so I jumped in with both feet. I bought the first season on DVD (though I did ask the clerk to put it in a brown wrapper) and started watching. After having consumed the entire first season and half the second, I must admit I've acquired a taste for *Desperate Housewives* that is perhaps not unlike Oprah's love for Krispy

Kreme Donuts. Yes, we know the show's not good for us, but it's so sinfully sweet and delicious, we can't help ourselves! And as someone who has all the plot summaries of *Gilligan's Island* committed to memory, I can't claim to stand on higher cultural ground. In fact, I now have a sort of sympathy, a fondness even, for the gals of Wisteria Lane. So come with me (intoned in the soothing angelic voice of dear departed Mary Alice) and meet the neighbors.

Susan Mayer (played by Teri Hatcher)

If, through some miracle of modern science, Lucy Ricardo and Mary Tyler Moore had ever had a child, it would be Susan. She's the lovely, yet bumbling girl next door whose plans "oft go awry." If she steps out of the house in nothing but a towel, you can be sure it will get caught in the door of a departing car. If she sneaks into a rival's home to see if her love interest is there, she sets the house on fire. All of Susan's life has a drama factor of Mach ten. And yet, her statistics are rather normal.

A divorcée raising a thirteen–going-on-thirty daughter (Julie), Susan works at home as a children's book illustrator. You know this because she will talk about "her agent" every so often, and at least once in the first season you see Susan with what appears to be a crayon in her hand. Most of the time, though, she works at her real full-time job—finding someone to love.

Susan is winsome, vulnerable, romantic, and clumsy, and has the hots for the hunky plumber, Mike Delfino. If this were a bird book, I would list her most identifying markings as: bra strap is always showing. Susan also has a penchant for clingy, loose-weave sweaters.

Bree Van De Kamp (played by Marcia Cross)

If you haven't met Bree, think Martha Stewart on steroids. If Susan is part Lucy/part Mary, Bree is the demon spawn of June Cleaver and Nancy Reagan. From her Marilyn Quayle flip to her stiletto-clad feet, Bree is the embodiment of carefully planned perfection. She is also the only one who appears to have an active faith life, but given her actions, you might think she's reading "The Gospel According to Emily Post."

For Bree, nothing is more enjoyable than a well-run dinner party, nothing more satisfying than polishing the good family silver. In one episode Bree, believing her son is on drugs, goes to her cupboard to get a suitable container for a urine sample. When she opens the cupboard, you see row upon row of carefully arranged containers—with the lids! When I saw that, I knew her son wasn't the only one on drugs.

A recent widow, Bree was married for eighteen years to Dr. Rex Van De Kamp. She has two average-looking children: Danielle (the president of the high school abstinence club) and Andrew (the recently out-of-the-closet troubled child). Bree doesn't work outside of the home, but her home is a piece of work. She is cool, caring, and capable—as handy with her rifle as she is with her food processor. You can spot Bree at a distance by her flaming red hair and the ever-present string of pearls that grace her slender neck. For sweaters, Bree favors cashmere sets in muted tones.

Gabrielle Solis (played by Eva Longoria)

Every neighborhood needs a sex kitten, and Wisteria Lane has one in the beautiful form of Gabrielle ("Gabby" to her Neanderthal husband). She is a former model turned housewife married to Carlos Solis, a rich and handsome Latino with a violent temper. To say that Gabrielle has a loose understanding of fidelity is an understatement. The first time I saw Gabrielle, she was licking the finger of her lawn boy lover (right before the dining room sex scene). Perhaps Gabrielle's most famous moment was the night she snuck home and mowed the lawn in her ball gown so Carlos wouldn't fire the gardener.

Gabrielle is remarkably self-aware—she knows full well she is shallow, greedy, and self-centered. But that's what makes her so darn lovable! Dressed in tiny bright outfits that suggest that Barbie is her personal shopper, Gabrielle is all about attracting attention—from her French manicure to her lacey lingerie. My ten-year-old niece said, "I want to be Gabrielle when I grow up because her clothes make me happy." If only they made Gabrielle happy.

When Gabrielle's not having sex, she's shopping, squaring off with Carlos, or jogging in one of her many pastel-colored running suits. (I didn't know that Victoria's Secret made athletic wear.) Beautiful, vain, passionate, and strangely loyal, Gabrielle puts the sizzle in this hot show. You'll quickly notice that Gabrielle has solved Susan's bra-strap "problem" by wearing strapless tops. When the weather gets cool, Gabrielle can be seen wearing off-the-shoulder shawl neck sweaters.

Lynette Scavo (played by Felicity Huffman)

A former hotshot advertising executive, Lynette seems to have drawn the short straw and now is an at-home mom with four rambunctious children. Her lovely house is usually littered with dishes, toys, and clutter. She struggles to find day care, get her children into the right school, keep her marriage exciting, and find time for herself. During season one, she became so obsessed with being the perfect mom that she started taking her son's ADD medication. Yet despite the drug use, she's the one with whom most women can easily, if reluctantly, identify. Let's face it. Everyone wants to be Gabrielle, but no one wants to be Lynette.

Married eight years to Tom, another advertising executive, who travels a lot, Lynette is competitive, harried, loving, jealous, and most of all, questioning. Susan doesn't seem to be self-aware enough to ask the larger questions. Lynette, on the other hand, knows exactly how she got where she is, but constantly wonders if she chose the right path. This questioning doesn't change, even when she and Tom trade places and Lynette heads back to the high-powered world of business.

In a bird-watcher's guide, I'd have to distinguish between "season one Lynette" (makeupless, sweat suit-wearing woman with baby spit on her shoulder) and "season two Lynette" (with makeup, Ann Taylor suit-wearing woman with baby spit on her shoulder). But even though her setting changes, she is just as harried and desperate as ever. If you're trying to spot Lynette, look for a flyaway dark blond shag and the buffest arms this side of Madonna. That's Lynette.

Edie Britt (played with gusto by Nicolette Sheridan)

Every garden of Eden has a serpent, and Wisteria Lane's comes slithering in the form of blond bombshell Edie Britt. Edie is so naughty she's lovable. Like Gabrielle, Edie is self-aware. She's a man-eater and she knows it, a true top-of-the-food chain predator. Edie's role in the show is clear: she's there to start trouble—and oh, the trouble she starts.

Watch as Edie comes outside in short shorts and a halter-top to wash her car! Gasp as Edie horns in on Susan's date! Laugh as Edie and Mrs. Huber trade barbs! Hiss as Edie tries to break up Susan and Mike by staging an "intervention!" Cringe as Edie reveals all of Susan's secrets to the evil Paul!

Perhaps because Edie is a secondary character, we don't see as much of her as the others. Or maybe it's because she's the only person who's not a housewife, having neither husband nor children. Or maybe it's because her successful real estate business keeps her away from Wisteria Lane. Considering her clothing choices are straight out of Frederick's of Hollywood,™ I'd imagine her "open houses" are quite popular.

If you're looking for Edie, figure out where the men are. Edie's sure to follow. As for sweaters, Edie eschews anything so modest, preferring to wear tops that allow full view of her undergarments. In other words, Edie makes Susan look Amish.

Mary Alice Young (played by Brenda Strong)

Like the narrator in *Our Town,* Mary Alice is our all-knowing guide to the people and plots of Wisteria Lane. Her luscious voice-overs start and end every show, framing the stories and interpreting the outcomes. Because Mary Alice is dead, we see her only in flashbacks, but it's easy to see why she fit in with the other women.

The keeper of a perfect house, immaculately dressed in slacks and sweater sets, Mary Alice Young had it all. Her husband, Paul, has one of those perfect TV jobs that leaves ample time for skulking around the neighborhood. Her son, Zach, starts out as a shy but normal teen before experiencing a severe mental breakdown. And who could blame him? But like so much on Wisteria Lane, Mary Alice's perfect life is not all it seems, and before the first episode is over, Mary Alice has committed suicide, Zach has started to act out, and Paul has clearly been identified as "the evil husband."

Betty Applewhite (played by Alfre Woodard)

Betty is a latecomer to Wisteria Lane, and relegated to a minor role. It's as if the producers of the show woke up one morning and slapped their heads, "We forgot about African Americans!" Enter Betty, the calm, cool black woman whose musical talents are matched only by her ability to handle a handgun.

Betty's style is elegant and mature, a sort of "Oprah meets Bea Arthur," which flatters her full figure. (Of course, on *Desperate Housewives* anything above a size 6 counts as full-figured.) She favors unstructured jackets, which allow for full maneuvering when she's wrestling her deviant son to the ground. Setting aside her race and size, Betty fits right in on Wisteria Lane. She loves her sons, keeps a beautiful house, and is up to her ears in mystery and scandal.

And the Rest...

I won't bother to introduce the men. They are important only insofar as they interact with the housewives. One interesting thing to note is that the men seem to be a little less exaggerated than the women, which makes them more sympathetic.

Also, a loony set of stock characters come in and out of the stories as necessary. There's self-righteous Mrs. Huber, the neighborhood blackmailer and busy body, who also happens to be the first person to self-identify as a Christian. There's Mrs.

McCluskey, Lynette's crotchety neighbor, whose bitter exterior hides a warm heart. There's Maisy Gibbons, the paragon of suburban virtue, who supplements her husband's income by turning tricks in the afternoons.

These are the major and minor players in this wickedly delightful comedy-drama. But one final character must be introduced—the setting. Wisteria Lane appears to exist in a hermetically sealed biosphere—like San Diego under glass. There is no weather besides pleasant sunshine (unless called for by the plot). Time doesn't even pass except in a jerky fictional way. You'll never see Gabrielle celebrate Christmas nor Betty light the Kwanzaa candles. Even days of the week are disguised. The houses are outlandishly large and perfectly, if blandly, decorated. The whole location is awash in warm light and vibrant colors, like a *Better Homes and Gardens* cover come to life. (The backlot on which Wisteria Lane is built is the same place used for *Leave it to Beaver*.[8] In fact, some people have told me that Bree's house is the actual Cleaver residence with a new façade. So that's where she got those pearls!)

Yet for all the variety the characters represent, there's little actual diversity on the show. There is a particular and carefully positioned point of view. *Desperate Housewives* is an upper–middle-class drama. The neighborhood and the houses are part of a vision of affluent suburbia that Americans idealize. From a statistical standpoint, very few of us live or can ever hope to live in such a lovely environment. But we seem to all have a vision of what constitutes the good life—and it looks a lot like Wisteria Lane.

Thus the particular trials and tribulations of our dear house-wives aren't really universal. Many women know what it's like to have to find a job, but it's the rare woman who can, like Gabrielle, march into a modeling agency and get work. (This is such an unreal moment…she's far too short to be a model.) Most of my friends with children know how hard it is to find good day care, but how many of us have had to search for the right live-in nanny?

Another fascinating piece of the *Desperate Housewives* scenario is that it's ultimately generic. Rooth, a theatre professor and professional costume designer, alerted me to this. She said, "Watch carefully. There's nothing specific about the show. There's nothing that points to a particular ethnicity, religion, or even region of the country. It's as if *Desperate Housewives* could be anywhere, and nowhere." Rooth believes this generic quality is so that anyone can project themselves onto the characters without the messy details of real life getting in the way. "It's as if the show is populated not by fully formed characters but by carefully constructed advertising demographics," Rooth said.

She has a point. We have the sexy Latina, the soccer mom, the lovelorn divorcée, and the traditional homemaker—each one a neat and discrete category with its own cultural assumptions and stereotypes. Don't you wonder if political strategists have started to use the housewives as shorthand in their planning meetings? "We're showing a three point lead among the 'Brees,' but we're trailing with the 'Lynettes.' Obviously, the election is in the hands of the 'Susans.'" (Lord, have mercy!)

On the surface the characters may look diverse, but don't let the hair color fool you. Economically and socially, they are all the same. (Looking at the *Desperate Housewives* cover of *Vanity Fair* I thought I was seeing an ad for Clairol. "What's your preference? Perfect Red Bree or Chestnut Susan?")

So if the world of Wisteria Lane is so rarified, why do 25 million of us tune in week after week? Maybe it's just because the show is stylish, well-acted campy fun. And like many forms of entertainment, it offers a moment's escape from the messier, duller stuff of real life. As my sister-in-law Nancy quipped, "It meets my only requirement for entertainment—it doesn't ask me to think!"

You have to admire the style of *Desperate Housewives*. The casting is perfect—it's been a long time since such a capable set of actors took on such an improbable show. That's part of the charm. Who but Nicolette Sheridan could pull off the ridiculous sexpot antics of Edie with a straight face? (There is room for a joke about Botox here, but I just can't bear to make it.) And who but Felicity Huffman could make parenting the Scavo monsters seem humanly possible? It's the talent of the main players that gives the stories more life and humanity than they deserve. Yet I suspect we watch *Desperate Housewives* not simply because it's fluffy entertainment.

Back to that regional conference meeting—Peggy, an artist from the East Coast, pulled me aside after a workshop. "I wanted to tell you about my favorite moment on *Desperate Housewives.*" She told me about the episode where Lynette starts taking her son's medicine to cope with the demands of being a housewife. At the end of the episode, Lynette, surrounded by her friends, is crying about what a failure she is as a mother. Then Bree confesses how awful she felt when she was home with her small children. Lynette cuts her off, demanding, "Why didn't you tell me?" After recounting the scene, Peggy, with tears in her eyes, said, "I know how Lynette feels. I've been right there."

Desperate Housewives is more than sudsy late-night entertainment. Against this hyper-stylized setting, these generically perfect characters wrestle with some of the same issues real women face every day. Granted, not many of us (I hope) have to cope with blackmailing neighbors or bodies popping up in the local reservoir. But as we watch Lynette try to be a good mother, or Bree try to forgive Rex's infidelity, or Susan try get Mike's attention, we nod knowingly. Like Peggy, we've been right there. Real life can sometimes make us very desperate.

CHAPTER 2

Is Zero Even a Size?

Let's say aliens land, having come from a far-off galaxy where there's nothing to do but watch prime time television emanating from a distant blue planet. Based on *Desperate Housewives* what do you think they'd expect women to look like? They'd expect women to be thin, physically fit and young...or at least young looking. Furthermore, I imagine they'd expect us all to have long straight hair, have a penchant for slip-on pumps, and be wearing clothes that are that rare combination of skin-tight yet ready to slip off with the least encouragement. (Aren't they going to be disappointed!)

Consider the following scene. Gabrielle, newly pregnant, is shopping for the right dress to impress her "model" girlfriends. The endearing gay clerk struggles to get a hot little blue number zipped up and finally says, "Maybe you should try the next size up. You want me to bring you the zero?" Gabrielle yells, "Are you saying I'm *fat*??"

Watching this scene nearly sent me into depression. First, anyone who's wearing size double zero (is zero even a number?)

15

should be forced to wear sneakers and plaid jumpers. Second, it is criminal to allow tiny actresses to "play pregnant." It constitutes false advertising. Yes, I admit that it's possible for a woman pregnant with her first child to remain svelte for a time. During my first pregnancy, I was cute until about the twenty-fifth week. Then overnight I morphed into a hippo on steroids, and a cranky hippo at that. With my second child, I was cute until about the twelfth week. With my third child, I wore maternity clothes the day after the stick turned pink. But then *Desperate Housewives* isn't big on realism when it comes to portraying women, regardless of age or stage of life. Let's take a closer look.

Lynette, who's had four children (the first two were twins), looks like she probably carried her children in a backpack rather than by the more conventional method. She signals her identity as a mother by wearing dumpy clothes, but they hang off a body that looks like those you see on late night infomercials for exercise machines.

Bree is wraith-thin and has thighs so trim that she can wear those tacky golf pants without looking like the seat covers of a '75 Pinto. This is a woman who wears pearls to garden, a woman whose wardrobe is so extensive that she is able to lay out ensembles in every color of the muted rainbow.

Susan, is small enough that she and her thirteen-year-old daughter can swap clothes, we learn in one episode. (I found this idea completely improbable. Julie wouldn't swap clothes with Susan because Julie has better sense.) Susan has an endless supply of cashmere ponchos, low-rider jeans, and lacey tank tops, none of which are sold at Lane Bryant.

And Gabrielle? My daughter said it best. "That lady looks like my Polly Pocket!" Polly Pockets are two-inch tall dolls with plastic slip-on clothes. I think the comparison is pretty apt, except it's much easier to get Gabby's clothes off.

Now I admit that some characters on *Desperate Housewives* are larger than size six, but usually they are the source of comic relief. The main one is dumpy Mrs. Huber, who is by turns the source of comedy and tragedy. In the end, she's so nasty that even her sister doesn't mourn her death. (Felicia Huber says of her sister, "I hated Martha. She was a wretched, pitiable woman, and the day she died, the world became a better place." How's that for sisterly devotion?)

The fact is that the average adult woman wears at least double digits. One of my more full-figured friends likes to remind me that Marilyn Monroe was supposed to have worn a luscious size sixteen. But you'd never see anyone that large in the center of the action on Wisteria Lane. What's even more troubling is that we never see these impossibly slim and trim women work out or go the gym, with the exception of Gabrielle, though I think her workouts aren't about caring for her body as much as displaying the goods.

I was curious about how "average-sized" women reacted to the skinny minis on *Desperate Housewives,* and was happy to discover that most women I talked to didn't get too worked up about it. Zella and Bonita, who work at a local church, would describe themselves as "full-figured gals," and yet they had no problems with it. Bonita said, "No one looks like that! It's totally unreal!" When I asked if watching the show made them uncomfortable about their own weight, they responded with a matter-of-fact, "no, of course not."

Lots of evidence suggests that our cultural preference for "thin" shapes and distorts how women see themselves. (Today's hot tabloid topic is whether or not Lindsay Lohan is bulimic— and whether or not that's a bad thing.) But when it comes to *Desperate Housewives* the attitude seems to be, it's just make-believe. Having the main characters be so impossibly thin moves the show out of the realm of actual life. There's nothing to feel bad about. It would be like getting depressed because you lacked Samantha Stephens's magic powers or Tinkerbell's wings.

One odd twist of realism in this otherwise unrealistic show is the portrayal of the teenagers. My friend Rooth alerted me to this. "Did you notice how homely the teenagers are? They look just like the kids that live in my house!" It was a real epiphany. With the possible exception of the boy toy John, the teenagers of Wisteria Lane are an amazingly average-looking group. Julie, Zach, Danielle, Andrew—this is not the gorgeous gang from *Dawson's Creek*. Look closely—you'll see signs of pimples and receding chins and odd hairstyles, just like you see at home.

Why would a show that worships the idol of youth and beauty cast such average-looking kids? Rooth has a theory. This show is aimed at adult women, not teenagers. And adult women don't want to be reminded they aren't dewy teens anymore. *Desperate Housewives* eliminates any competition in focus by making the teenagers look like, well, teenagers. This show is about the mothers, not their children, and those mothers are hot!

The same aesthetic is at work in the men. Tom, Carlos, Rex, and George are pretty normal looking. They're not out of shape, but neither are they the sort of buff and beefy men who usually populate prime time. Even the hunks, Mike and John, aren't displayed to full advantage. In some ways the men are like the male chorus line featured in the Miss America pageant dance numbers: generically and neutrally attractive so as not to steal the spotlight from the girls.

But what about age? The ladies of Wisteria Lane aren't just thin; they are young—or at least timeless. They appear to be, as Auntie Mame described her best friend, Vera, "somewhere between forty and death."[1]

An actress I know once complained, "As far as Hollywood goes, if you're thirty, you're invisible." So when I first heard about *Desperate Housewives,* I was delighted to see that the cast was "mature"—the term we now use since "middle-aged" has become a dirty word. All the actresses are (appropriately) in their forties, with the exception of Eva Longoria. Yet this is one dirty secret the show doesn't want to reveal.

Case in point; Edie meets Betty Applewhite's son for the first time, and he calls her "ma'am." Edie sneers (as much as she can with that flat upper lip) and says, "I'm not old enough to be called 'ma'am.' That's a term you use for an older woman, a woman like," pointing over the hedge at Susan, "her." Message received loud and clear: old is bad.

Another scene involves an exchange between Susan and her ditzy mother, Sophie. Sophie has brought a couple of "gentlemen" home to party, and Susan tells her mother to get rid of them. Sophie refuses, and Susan hisses, "Either you get those men out of my house or I'm going to tell them how old you really are!" Sophie hustles the men out the door.

Any doubt about this "ageism?" Ask yourself, who's the evil neighbor who's always after Lynette's boys? The aged and cranky Mrs. McCluskey. Who tries to ruin Gabrielle's life? Her nasty old mother-in-law, Mrs. Solis. Still doubt the ageism? Watch carefully and you'll see that not one birthday above the age of eight is celebrated in the entire first season. Time may be passing in my life, but not for the women of Wisteria Lane.

If the writers of *Desperate Housewives* were going to play true to life, there would be talk of the "big M," menopause. Gather more than four "mature" women together in my church, and you'll get the lowdown on hot flashes, weight gain, and the other delightful gifts of menopause and its cousin, peri-menopause. Talk about the stuff of dark comedy. My sister-in-law Eileen once said, "I don't mind getting older. I just wish everything would stop moving south."

Wouldn't it be great if one of the housewives started into menopause? Frankly, I'd like to see chilly Bree experience a real hot flash, and discover the downside to close-fitting cashmere. Chances are their contracts have a "no menopause" clause, because everyone knows older actresses don't work.

Okay, there was a time when, faced with yet another cast of perfectly coifed and clothed actresses, I would slip into a true feminist rant, denouncing in detail the evil effects of sexist patriarchy, perhaps concluding with a call to boycott the show, or at least send a sharply worded e-mail during the commercial breaks. Yet time and experience have taught me that there's nothing new or sinister about our culture's love of youth and beauty. We have always grasped at those shiny idols. And when one golden calf falls, another rises up to take its place. That's the way of the world. I survived Marcia Brady. I survived Suzanne

Sommers. I survived Carrie Bradshaw. I can handle Susan Mayer. And I do it, in part, through faith.

Andrea, a "mature" dreadlock-wearing minister, relates this tale. "I was sitting having lunch with my friend, and these two women came in, hair all straight, wearing these fabulous tight clothes. I watched them fuss their way to a table and I said, 'Thank God I've given up being glamorous! It's too much work.'" Now Andrea is capable of stopping traffic—her ability to attract male attention is near Edie-esque—but not because she looks like she lives on Wisteria Lane. Ask her what her secret is, and she'll tell you, "I'm finally comfortable being who I am."

You may think this is self-talk, but I see her words as a bold theological statement. For Andrea, being comfortable with who she is means accepting the person God created her to be and knowing that, from the standpoint of faith, beauty comes from the inside, regardless of the external package.

From a biblical perspective, beauty is difficult to define or evaluate. Song of Solomon celebrates the beauty of the female body, but I dare anyone to go to the gym and tell the trainer, "I want my belly to look like 'a heap of wheat, encircled with lilies' and my breasts to look like a couple of baby gazelles" (see Song 7:2–3). Or shall we take fashion tips from the Paul? "For if a woman will not veil herself, then she should cut off her hair" (1 Cor. 11:6a). How about Peter? "Do not adorn yourselves outwardly by braiding your hair and by wearing gold ornaments or fine clothing" (1 Pet. 3:3). Paul, who prefers women to keep their heads covered and their mouths closed, would have a stroke if he saw *Desperate Housewives*.

Proverbs 31:10–31 gives a description of the perfect woman. This passage, usually translated as "a capable wife" but better translated as "a virtuous woman", gives us no clear picture of what a woman is supposed to *look like*, only what she's supposed to do. She cooks, she weaves, she sews, she manages the household, buys and sells real estate, trades in the market, cares for the poor. She's the Martha Stewart of the ancient world; no wonder no one can find her! The text may not tell us what she looks like, but I know. She looks exhausted.

In fact, Song of Solomon aside, scripture shows a deep suspicion of beauty. Show me a woman in the Bible whose primary descriptor is "beautiful" and I'll show you trouble. David didn't invite Bathsheba up to his room because he liked the way she prayed (2 Sam. 11:2–5). Herod didn't give Salome the head of John the Baptist as a reward for her piety (Mt. 14:6–12; Mk. 6:22–29). Jacob's preference for Rachel over Leah had nothing to do with Rachel's compassion for the poor (Gen. 29:9–12). (Reading the passage in Genesis where Laban tricks Jacob by slipping Leah into the marriage bed, and Jacob doesn't notice he's got the wrong girl until morning, caused one woman in my Bible study to mutter, "Men!") The Bible seems to say, if all you are is beautiful, there's not much to you.

Think about the matriarchs of the faith, women such as Mary, Sarah, or Elizabeth. We don't know if they were beautiful. What we know is that they were faithful—and that's what really matters. The last lines of Proverbs 31 speak the truth: "Charm is deceitful, and beauty is vain, / but a woman who fears the LORD is to be praised" (Prov. 31:30).

The gift of faith (and age) is learning to see myself as God sees me, from the inside, with the eyes of love. The people I know who are really beautiful are not anxious about age or size. They take care of themselves, but not in a life-and-death battle against the ravages of time. Perhaps they understand the wisdom of Proverbs 31:30: youth and beauty are fleeting gifts.

The *Desperate Housewives* may live in a world untouched by time, but we live in the real world, a world of stretch marks, fad diets, bad hair days and laugh lines. We live in a world where women and men come in all shapes and sizes, and size double zero was probably left behind in fourth grade. We know that even Gabrielle's assets will head south some day (I hope I live long enough to see it), but a healthy acceptance of who you are in the eyes of God—beloved and capable—is the gift that endures, the real beauty that time cannot change.

CHAPTER 3

For Better, for Worse...and for Now

If I ever decide to enter a more lucrative profession, I think I'd like to be a marriage counselor on *Desperate Housewives*. Not only would I have as many clients as my couch could hold (especially since George pushed Dr. Goldfine off a bridge), but the problems of these couples are wildly entertaining. They put the "fun" in dysfunctional.

Among my clients would be the likable Lynette and Tom, overwhelmed by raising four children, struggling for power at home and at work. Lynette is always on the lookout for signs of trouble in her marriage. Tom is always on the lookout for signs of trouble in Lynette. Bree's Martha Stewart-like quest for perfection drives her husband into the arms of a neighborhood prostitute (a woman who is not averse to using a whip). But when Rex's betrayal is revealed, Bree discovers what keeps couples together—a desire for revenge. On the other side of the coin, Gabrielle's marriage to Carlos is founded on greed and lust, and marked by infidelity. But when the going gets tough, the Solises are surprised to discover that they actually love each other. And Susan, whose first marriage ended in what can only be described as a traditional divorce, is looking for love in all the wrong places.

Obviously, marriage isn't portrayed as a particularly positive experience on *Desperate Housewives*. This leads some conservative critics to rant about how the show undermines traditional marriage by casting marriage in such a cynical light. The exploits and antics of Wisteria Lane are, some contend, a gross and demoralizing exaggeration of the sacred institution of marriage. But the truth is, in my experience, *Desperate Housewives* is not that far from reality.

Because of our role in preparing for and officiating at weddings, no group is more jaded about the institution of marriage than mainline Christian ministers. We've seen too much, counseled too many couples, and heard too many confessions. There was the couple who almost didn't marry because they couldn't agree on where to have one another's names tattooed. There was the groom who refused to sublet his bachelor apartment, because "a guy needs his space." There was the wedding coordinator who suggested the baptismal font be moved to a storeroom because "it doesn't work visually." There was the wedding party who, at the conclusion of the service, did tequila shots on the steps of the church before climbing into a stretch SUV headed to the reception. No wonder most pastors would rather do a funeral than a wedding. (Asked why this is so, one of my friends said, "You get less backchat from the participants.")

Because of our experiences, pastors also understand that these surface problems are just symptoms of deeper issues. The real problem with the institution of marriage, as a covenanted relationship ordained by God, is that it involves people—broken, self-centered, sinful people. Given human sinfulness, it's amazing that any marriage lasts a lifetime. Perhaps we should stop wringing our hands and, instead, rejoice that *only* half of marriages end in divorce.

Yet there are Christians who don't accept human brokenness as the source of the problem. Instead, they decry the sorry state of marriage in the United States and claim that "traditional marriage" is being undermined by outside forces. Birth control, the women's movement, no-fault divorce laws, and permissive liberal culture have all been blamed for the decline in traditional marriage. The latest scapegoat is same-sex unions, and all across the country a call is arising from the right to stop this "outrageous practice." In December of 2005, a "pastors' summit" was convened in St. Paul, Minnesota, with the sole purpose of figuring out how to get an anti-gay marriage amendment on the 2006 ballot. "Protect traditional marriage!" was the rallying cry. Call me crazy, but I doubt that keeping same-sex couples from marrying will decrease divorce rates among heterosexuals. That's like banning people of color from your country club in hopes of improving your golf game.

The problem with "protecting traditional marriage" is that we have no clear understanding of what traditional marriage looks like. Certainly scripture doesn't offer a detailed description of "traditional marriage." Looking through the Old Testament, we might surmise that the primary purpose of marriage was for the orderly exchange of property. Marriage was an important economic relationship, a contract through which a woman was transferred from one man to another and a woman's economic future was secured. (Ever wonder where the words "to have and to hold from this day forward" came from? Old English property law, that's where.)

Look through the Old and New Testaments—you'll be hard pressed to find a clear guide for the model marriage that isn't based on an unequal, patriarchal relationship. Women were considered property—cherished and valued, yes, but property nonetheless. Which is why the Israelites are instructed in the Ten Commandments not to covet any of the neighbor's property—not his house, wife, slave, ox, or donkey (Ex. 20:17). I hope this list isn't in order of importance.

The New Testament isn't any clearer on the subject. Jesus himself doesn't say much about marriage, though the Christian tradition holds that he sanctifies marriage by performing the first miracle at the wedding in Cana. (One scholar thinks this is a ridiculous interpretation, quipping, "That's like saying the healing of the Gerasene demoniac [in Mk. 5] sanctifies cemeteries.") Jesus' most famous words on marriage have to do with divorce. "Whoever divorces his wife and marries another commits adultery against her; and if she divorces her husband and marries another, she commits adultery" (Mk. 10:11–12). It's important to note that in Matthew's version, we suddenly have grounds for a divorce—*porneia*—which we ambiguously translate as "unchastity." This indicates that Jesus' teaching was being interpreted and altered by the earliest Christian communities.

Paul has some thoughts on the subject of marriage, but his opinions are bound by culture and time. As he writes in Ephesians, "Wives, be subject to your husbands as you are to the Lord. For the husband is the head of the wife just as Christ is the head of the church, the body of which he is the Savior" (Eph. 5:22–23). Not all contemporary women are interested in a relationship where the man is the unchallenged head of the household even if the husband does promise to honor and care for his mate. Among more conservative Christians, there is a belief that this Pauline model of marriage is the right one and offers the best chance of enduring marital bliss. Unfortunately, there is no evidence to support this. In fact, the divorce rate is slightly higher among people who belong to conservative Christian denominations.[1]

If biblical models of marriage offer little guidance to modern couples, then current popular culture offers even less. Our understanding of marriage has moved from an economic model to an emotional one. In other words, we marry for love, or rather, a particular vision of romantic love in which one relationship is supposed to meet all our needs: spiritual, emotional, psychological, and sexual. This is a huge burden for one relationship (one person) to bear, but that's what we seem to be expecting when we are looking for Mr. (or Ms.) Right.

This utopian vision of marriage is the kind of thing they used to talk about on *Sex and the City.* Marriage was the undiscovered country, the land of stability, happiness, security, and fulfillment. In some ways, *Desperate Housewives* reveals the dark truth behind this fantasy. A very wise person once said to me, "Getting married is easy. Being married is hard."

Yet as dysfunctional as the marriages are on *Desperate Housewives,* they're not without some merit. If you look closely, you can find some redeeming features, even some practical things any couple can do to strengthen their relationship. For example, good communication is essential for any healthy relationship. I love the way Tom and Lynette communicate about anything and everything, though not always effectively. One funny episode involved their new nanny, Claire. Tom accidentally sees Claire naked, and Lynette questions him about whether or not he finds her "too attractive." Tom thinks that Lynette is overreacting, and questions whether or not she really trusts him. These characters model pretty good communication skills in this scene. (Of course, for all Tom's protests, it turns out he's not being honest about how he feels. But when he catches himself ogling Claire's breasts at the dinner table, Tom takes the bull by the horns—or perhaps some other part of the bull—and lets the nanny go.)

Another aspect of a healthy relationship is expressing mutual respect and admiration for each other. On Wisteria Lane, this can take some strange forms, but you'll still see signs of it. In the midst of all their troubles, Rex overhears Bree scold their son, Andrew, for disrespecting Rex. No matter what has happened, Bree says, "Rex is the love of my life." Later, when Andrew pushes his mother out of his way with his foot, Rex storms into the room and, grabbing Andrew by the collar, hisses, "Don't let me ever catch you treating your mother like that again!" Now granted, these two moments are a little extreme, but they serve as epiphanies for Rex and Bree.

Yes, there are a few good marital moments on Wisteria Lane, but there are bad moments too. One problem is the way men are treated. One of the clearest messages of season one was "men cannot be trusted." My sister put it well: "For men, the show's like the Iranian court system—you're guilty until proven innocent." One of my favorite lines occurred when the girls were trying to get Susan to open Mike's letter, the one where he supposedly explained everything about his shady past. "Do you think he's telling the truth?" asks Susan. Bree retorts, "Think about how good men are at lying on the spot. God forbid you should give them time and a pen."

My other complaint is much more serious: *Desperate Housewives* places no value on fidelity. For instance, Gabrielle's affair with John is exciting and thrilling. When Mama Solis discovers her "dirty little secret" Gabrielle is not filled with remorse, but with anxiety about what Carlos will do if he finds out. When Tom's father (played by the eternally cute Ryan O'Neal) is caught having an affair, Lynette is furious. She asks him to explain himself, and he tells her he's done nothing wrong. "I've stayed married to a woman I don't love because I made a vow to God." (That's called obeying the letter, not the spirit, of the law.)

Someone will surely point out that the problem lies not with *Desperate Housewives,* but with the general state of affairs in our society. Infidelity is rampant, so much so that it's lost its power to shock us, so much so that it is a source of comedy rather than tragedy in popular culture. In fact, wearing a wedding ring no longer keeps potential suitors at bay. Instead, it's like dumping chum in the water—the sharks soon come circling. As a male friend of mine said, "If I had known how many women would hit on me after marriage, I'd have worn a wedding ring earlier." My problem is that *Desperate Housewives* makes infidelity look exciting and uncomplicated, far more lively than staying with the same boring person.

In the end, married love seems like an impossible dream on *Desperate Housewives,* and eventually everyone has to settle for something else. When Bree agrees to marry George the pharmacist, she explains to her friends that while she doesn't love him, she does find him to be a good companion. "True love is great, but at this point in my life, I think I'd rather go to the opera," she says. And when Gabrielle's affair with John is finally revealed, Carlos is furious. They fight about whose fault it is, and at the end, Gabrielle finally says, "When we got married, I thought we'd be so happy. Thank God we're still rich."

Interestingly enough the problem with popular culture's understanding of marriage is the same problem as the traditional biblical understanding of marriage: both treat the spouse as a possession. The only difference is that whereas women once were treated like livestock, now we treat our spouses like handbags, just another thing that enhances our image. It's not just a problem for women, but for men too.

Consider Carlos and Gabrielle. Their marriage provides both of them with external validation. Carlos wanted a trophy wife, a sign of his success and a source of envy for his business colleagues. Gabby needed Carlos's money to provide her with the opulent life she dreamed for herself. Plenty of couples marry for similar reasons.

I saw this same attitude when I was in college. Some of my friends owned stacks of *Bride's Magazine.* In their leisure time, they would leaf through the photos of beautiful brides, dreaming of the day they would get married. It was a goal to which they aspired without any idea of what it meant to be married. They were creating a list of things to acquire: the dress, the shoes, the ring, and the flowers. Then you pick out the man and voilà! You've got yourself a wedding! The groom is just another perfect possession.

Shannon, who teaches theology, describes it this way: "We see possessions as just another aspect of us, a way for us to shore up our external image of who we are." When we view a spouse (or love, for that matter) as just another thing to acquire, something that enhances our ideal vision of ourselves, we're heading for disaster. That's not the nature of real love. And while the Bible doesn't provide us with a handbook for marriage, it does teach us about the nature of real love.

The most popular scripture reading at weddings turns out to be the key to this puzzle. First Corinthians 13, which most wedding-goers can recite in their sleep, is actually a radical bit of theology.

> Love is patient; love is kind; love is not envious or boastful or arrogant or rude. It does not insist on its own way; it is not irritable or resentful; it does not rejoice in wrongdoing, but rejoices in the truth. It bears all things, believes all things, hopes all things, endures all things. Love never ends. (1 Cor. 13:4–8a)

This is not Paul's advice to newlyweds on the nature of romantic love. No. Paul is speaking about what sustains true Christian community, the soil out of which all our relationships grow—the love of God. This perfect love comes only from God, who *is* love. This is the love that flows into our lives *and* the model for how we are to love one another, especially in marriage. What Paul offers is a vision of love that is radically nonpossessive, the answer to our modern predicament.

What does nonpossessive love look like? Well, you won't find any of it on Wisteria Lane. Such love is risky, because it allows the spouse to be wholly other, without seeking to control or diminish him or her. Nonpossessive love is a gift that we give to our mate, not something we expect to get. It is a love grounded not in physical attraction or some other human value. Instead, it is grounded in the understanding that both of you are held in the hands of God, beloved and cherished. Nonpossessive love is not something you have; it is a way of being, and of seeing your mate.

This Christian understanding of love as nonpossessive offers us two things that can help us with marriage. One is a standard to aim for and judge by. Real love—the kind that Jesus offers—is selfless and life-giving. This is love that nurtures, supports, and heals. We are called to embody this kind of love in all our relationships, but most especially in our primary relationship. Unfortunately, some relationships not only don't embody such love—they actively deny and destroy love. That's why divorce is not just a fact of modern life; sometimes it's a necessity. No person, man or woman, should remain in a marriage that damages or threatens them, no matter how we interpret the words of Jesus.

The second thing the Christian tradition offers us is a vision of a greater love within which all other loves rest. In other words the love of God is the ground out of which all other loves grow. This is good news, because the truth about marriage is that even the best ones fall on hard times.

Around the time I got married, I heard about a couple in our church who were celebrating their seventieth anniversary. When someone asked the wife what the secret was to staying married so long, she said, "Well, I don't know. It wasn't always easy. I can't pretend there weren't some hard years. But you just trust it will get better." The phrase "hard years" struck me, because at 23, I couldn't imagine putting up with anyone who made me miserable for a month, let alone a whole year.

Every couple faces trials and tribulations in the course of a marriage, moments when you really wonder if you've married the right person. The causes of most fights are mundane: childcare, housework, money, and sex. But these small things can turn into major problems, such as adultery and abuse. The beauty and power of Christian love is that it helps us endure the bumps and shocks of life and trust that things will get better.

For those of us striving to be married in a world where scripture doesn't provide a road map for marriage and popular culture leads us to places like Wisteria Lane, the Christian faith offers real promise. We have the assurance of the love of God, who is the real love of our life. And this love provides the source, model, and context for our human relationships. This is great news because romantic love ebbs and flows, but God's love endures forever. Love, writ large, can hold us together when love, writ small, wears thin.

CHAPTER 4

Children—the Perfect Accessory

When we talk about children we're really talking about parenting, and in the case of *Desperate Housewives,* that means motherhood. I hesitate to say any more, because motherhood is such a loaded topic, tapping into many deeply held defenses, insecurities, ideals, and expectations, even for people who have no children. Anyone who chirps brightly about motherhood is skipping rope through a minefield. It's best to tread carefully, trying not to detonate any bombs.

Yet *Desperate Housewives* blunders right ahead, treating parenting as a hobby more than as a calling. The mothers of Wisteria Lane are little more than broad caricatures of socially constructed stereotypes. It's like watching Kabuki theatre— everyone in stylized makeup and costume. There is "Perfect Mother" Bree. She's probably read all the baby books, can quote Dr. Spock chapter and verse, and had her children using the toilet before they could walk. And as the perfect mother, she expects perfect children, which is why Andrew and Danielle cause her so much grief.

Then we have "Best Friend Mother," the hip and helpless Susan. In the course of Susan's divorce, she and Julie switched roles, as Julie reminds her mother: "Since dad left, I've been the mother. I cleaned the house, paid the bills. I even made my own doctor's appointments!" Julie is the voice of reason in the Mayer household, offering her mother counsel, support, and even advice about sex. They share confidences and clothes, and treat each other as equals, which is a perfect arrangement, until Julie needs a mother.

Then there is Lynette, "Stay-at-Home Mother." In the first season, Lynette is always dressed in sweats, looking harried and frantic. Overwhelmed and underappreciated, Lynette can't bring herself to discipline her beloved and challenging children. So her three boys ride roughshod over their mom, and terrorize the neighborhood. In Lynette, our fears about stay-at-home mothers are confirmed—they've traded success at work for failure at home.

Yet for all the exaggeration, there is a ring of authenticity to the parenting scenarios, something that resonates deep within us. The truth is, parenting is not for sissies. It's like the ultimate extreme sport, demanding every bit of strength, creativity, and cunning we can muster.

My sister-in-law Nancy, a truly inspired mother, had a daughter who threw epic fits in her early years. If she didn't get what she wanted, Abby would kick and scream until her demands were met. One day, as Abby began to yell in a store, Nancy took her by the shoulders and gently moved her to the side. "There. I think if you move over just a little bit to the left, then everyone in the whole store can hear you. Or maybe you'd like to stand on a chair for better effect?"

I'm not quite up to Nancy's creative standards, but when my oldest son was three and suffering from nightmares, we were at wits' end trying to get him to sleep through the night. We tried music, a nightlight, a series of stuffed animals—nothing worked. Finally, woken out of bed once again, I stumbled into his room and asked, "What in the world are you afraid of?" "The monsters that might try to get me," he whimpered. I went over to his toy chest and pulled out his plastic sword and shield. Handing them to him, I said, "Ok, now you're armed. I think you can take 'em." He smiled and slept soundly. Who knew?

Parenting is like the Peace Corps—it's the toughest job you'll ever love. Children have the power to transform us, which is why we go to such lengths to have them. (I hope none of us go the "Mary Alice" route in buying a baby and later believing we need to commit murder to keep the baby.)

Here I have a confession to make. As much as I love being a mother, I hate being pregnant. I realize this is wrong, that women are supposed to glow with maternal pride, rejoicing in all the incredible changes that are part of the miracle of bringing a new life into the world. But I never really got in touch with the "earth mother" side of me. Instead, I resent pregnancy and behave like I'm carrying Rosemary's baby. Ten days before our third child was born, we were at a family reunion at a lake resort. As I was waddling back to the car to leave, a kindly old gentleman came up and said, "I was talking with your father-in-law, and he told me he was expecting another grandson soon. I'll bet you're the mommy!" I rounded on him with remarkable speed for someone shaped like a giant pear and sneered, "Ya *think*?!"

The price we pay for having children doesn't end after delivery. Children tax our minds ("Why are oranges orange?"), our strength (putting hard shoes on a limp two-year-old could be an Olympic sport), our hearts (you never get over the first "I hate you!"), and even our stomachs (being sprayed with various bodily fluids—and solids—comes with the territory). And frankly, I never imagined I'd become the kind of person who would willingly wipe another person's nose with the inside of my shirt. Yet for our children, we willingly sacrifice sleep, money, youthful figures, time, careers, and even dignity.

In the world of Wisteria Lane, only Lynette seems to have made big sacrifices for her children, and her struggles are the most poignant and true to life. Whether she's worrying about how good a job the nanny does, arguing with Tom about spanking, or squaring off with Mrs. McCluskey, we knowingly nod our heads. And in the climactic scene in season one where Lynette cries, "I love my kids so much. I'm just sorry they have to have me as their mother!" we gasp, for she has said aloud what many of us have thought in our hearts.

Secretly, every mother suspects she's a failure. If we turn to the "experts" looking for advice and reassurance, we discover there *are* no real experts. You can always find someone who thinks you're doing it wrong. The choices start the minute the baby is born. Breast or bottle? Should infants sleep with parents or in a separate room? Should you feed on demand or put the baby on a schedule? Does early potty training lead to better brain development or just drive you up the wall? If you were to lay all the parenting experts end to end, they would point in all directions. As I once heard, "Parenting is the last bastion of the amateur."

All this self-doubt and questioning create such anxiety that we turn on one another. This is parenting as a competitive sport, in which we pit our choices against the choices of others, measuring the relative success (or failure) of our children to determine the winner. Why else do we cheer when Bree's son ends up in a boot camp for delinquent teens? Why else do we applaud when Lynette reveals that the popular birthday child is "patient zero" for the lice epidemic?

My husband, Neil, and I have friends who are perfect parents, and for years we endured the perfect behavior of their children. These weren't just good kids; these were Stepfordlike children who never talked back, never disobeyed, never disappointed. Compared with them, my children looked like they'd been raised by the Manson family. So when their eldest daughter came home from a mission trip with a tattoo, I was secretly overjoyed. Each new piercing, each new brush with the law brought me perverse satisfaction, some twisted reassurance that, by comparison, I was doing a fine job raising my children.

My sorry attitude reveals a pernicious myth about parenting, a myth that *Desperate Housewives* reinforces, namely, that good parenting guarantees good children. Or, as Proverbs 22:6 puts it, "Train children in the right way, and when old, they will not stray." Nothing could be farther from the truth, for children come with their own agendas. Some succeed despite less than adequate parenting. Some struggle even with a perfect upbringing. Most manage to thrive despite their parents. And in the end, parents cannot take credit for their children's successes...or their failures.

Part of what gives life to the myth of parents' being able to determine their children's success is the same possessiveness that taints our understanding of marriage. Like our spouses, our children can become extensions of ourselves, part of the way we want the world to see us. Good children, like the perfect accessory, enhance our image. Bad children cause us shame. Who hasn't leaned over to a misbehaving child and hissed, "Stop it! You're embarrassing me!" This is why Bree doesn't tell anyone where Andrew has gone; it makes her look bad.

Search the biblical text and you'll find all sorts of parents, good and bad. There's David (2 Sam. 18), the parent who loves his child so much he can't bear to put any limits on him, and as a result Absalom ends up hanging from a tree by his hair, only to be hacked to death by his father's servants. (David's anguished cry speaks for all parents who lose a child, "Would I had died instead of you, O Absalom, my son, my son!" [2 Sam. 18.33]). Worried about choosing your career over the well-being of your children? Consider the cautionary tale of Jephthah (Judg. 11:29–40), who, in exchange for career advancement, inadvertently ends up sacrificing his only daughter as an offering to the Lord. How about Rebekah, the mother who plays favorites? (Gen. 27). She cheats her eldest child out of his inheritance in order to secure the future for her favorite boy, and then never sees him again. And then there is father Abraham, a man so frighteningly faithful that he comes within a knife's strike of killing his only child (Gen. 22). As a preacher, I extol the faithfulness of Abraham; as a mother, I abhor it.

But of all the parents I find in scripture, my hero is the Canaanite woman in Matthew's gospel (Mt. 15:21–28). Recall the story. Jesus and the disciples are passing through the district of Tyre and Sidon, probably trying to attract as little attention as possible, and suddenly a foreign woman appears, shouting out, "Have mercy on me, Lord, Son of David, my daughter is tormented by a demon." (v. 22) This is a risky act, for in ancient times, women weren't supposed to speak to men in public, and foreigners and Jews did not interact. She keeps after him until Jesus calls out, "I was sent only to the lost sheep of the house of Israel." (v. 24) But this mother won't take no for an answer. Breaking the social conventions of the day, maybe even risking her life, she pushes through the disciples and kneels at Jesus' feet. "Lord, help me." (v. 25) "It is not fair to take the children's food and throw it to the dogs," Jesus replies. (v. 26) In the face of this cruel insult, she responds, "Yes, Lord, yet even the dogs eat the crumbs that fall from their masters' table." (v. 27) Jesus answers, "Woman, great is your faith! Let it be done for you as you wish." (v. 28) And her daughter is healed.

What a remarkable moment this is! This Canaanite mother risks everything—her dignity, her reputation, even her safety—to save her child. Furthermore, she knows she is worthy of Jesus' attention, and because of her faith, her daughter is healed.

Study this woman carefully and you'll see the central claim—or demand—of the Christian faith lived out in its entirety. Jesus Christ teaches his followers to be self-possessing and other-centered. In other words, we must first claim our true identity as a child of God. Then, once we understand that we have value apart from anything we have or anything we do, then, and only then, are we able to faithfully serve others. (Why else does Jesus tell us to love our neighbors as we love ourselves?) In this Christian framework, there's no place for martyr mommies, those self-denying women at the heart of bad jokes. (Q: How many Jewish mothers does it take to change a light bulb? A: Oh, don't trouble yourself. I'll just sit here in the dark.) We are called to care for ourselves as well as for others. Which reminds me of the best parenting advice I ever heard—from a flight attendant: "Secure your own oxygen mask before assisting a child."

Yet there's another myth about parenting that operates on *Desperate Housewives,* the myth of "the big moment." Over lunch with Zach, Susan has to decide if she will bring him back to Mike (his real father) or if she will send him away, thus protecting Julie from Zach's obsessive attention. Bree and Rex argue about whether or not Andrew should have to quit the swim team as a punishment for running over Mama Solis. Explaining why he's against it, Rex says, "I'm not going to ruin his future!" When Lynette wants to get rid of her son's pretend friend, symbolized by an old-fashioned umbrella, she worries he will never forgive her.

These are "big moments in parenting," in which the health and happiness of the child hangs in the balance. Cue the tense music! Don't make a mistake, mom and dad! This is it! What *are* you going to *do* ?

In Christian terms, this is *kairos*—the ripe moment. *Kairos,* a Greek word that describes qualitative time, is about the fullness of time, the coming together of all things, and ultimately, the coming of the Lord. *Kairos* is "the big moment." What *are* you going to do? *Desperate Housewives* makes parenting look like a drama, a series of kairotic moments. No wonder those women are desperate.

The other concept of time in the Christian tradition is *chronos,* meaning normal, human time. A Greek term that describes quantitative time, *chronos* is the ticking of the clock, the changing of seasons, the everyday passing of time.

In the real world, parenting is not about *kairos,* but *chronos.* It's putting a meal on the table, showing up for the school play, and driving the team to Little League practice. It's about wiping noses, packing lunches, checking homework, and setting limits. It's reading "The Little Engine that Could" for the 300th time even though the prose is wretched and the illustrations appalling. It's remembering to put peanut butter on both pieces of the bread so the jelly won't leak. It's never saying, "I told you so" when that career as a rock musician doesn't pan out. It's loving our children enough, day by day, to let them become who God means them to be rather than some extension of our own fragile ego.

Parenting is all about *chronos,* and there are times when we get so tired of the day-to-day work and worry of parenting that we wonder if it makes any difference at all. But there's one more miraculous thing about being a parent. When it comes to parenting, the *chronos is* the *kairos.*[1] All those sandwiches and late nights, all those art projects and ball games add up so that our children can move into the world as whole people who know they are loved. The big moment in parenting is just the sum of all the little moments over the course of a lifetime. As a friend of mine once said, "With parenting the days are long, but the years are short."

CHAPTER 5

Working Girls

Careers on network television go in and out of vogue. There was a time when everyone was following Darrin Stephens (you remember *Bewitched?*) into advertising. Then it was journalism, always a popular TV career, probably because it appears to give you lots of money and unlimited free time (see *Sex and the City* or *Everybody Loves Raymond* for reference.) Lately, everyone is a doctor, a lawyer, or a crime scene investigator. (Can I just say that on *Grey's Anatomy* the doctors have so much sex that I'm starting to think it must be on the Board Exams.)

On Wisteria Lane, though, nobody works, not even the employed. Having a job is like going to school for the younger set—something to get you off stage while the *real* action goes on. Now, some fans will surely cry out that at least three of the girls have careers (unless you count Gabrielle's "modeling") but let's be serious. Edie is a real estate agent who dresses like a hooker. Buy a house from Edie and, instead of the traditional "walk through," you get the less traditional "vamp through."

Susan is supposed to be a children's book illustrator, and in one episode we actually see her with paper. But no one that clumsy should be trusted with pastels. Then there's Lynette, whose season two return to the fast track of advertising is the dramatic vehicle that drives her character. The best thing about advertising is that it allows Lynette to wear fabulous suits and make dramatic pitches to large groups of people in glass-walled conference rooms. The careers on *Desperate Housewives* remind me of the careers my Barbies had when I was a child. Malibu Barbie was a supermodel veterinarian, while Classic Barbie was a ballet dancer who sat on the bench of the Fifth Circuit Court. (Skipper, whose clothes were not nearly so cool, chose to stay at home and keep house for her more glamorous sister.)

Here is where *Desperate Housewives* departs most sharply from life as I know it. In the real world, most women work. According to U.S. Department of Labor statistics, 60 percent of American women work outside the home. This figure jumps to 72 percent if you look at single mothers. Almost half of two-parent households have both parents in the outside workforce.[1] For most of us, dealing with the challenges and complications of work life isn't a minor subplot—it's the main event. This is why Lynette's story line is so popular. She is the only character who is juggling work and family issues, usually for humorous effect.

One of my favorite moments occurred early in the second season, when Lynette was interviewing for a job. Because of a babysitter breakdown, Lynette ends up taking her infant daughter to the agency and leaving her in the less-than-capable hands of the office receptionist. As Lynette makes her big pitch, she sees her daughter crying out in the lobby, unattended. When she can stand it no longer, Lynette excuses herself, gets her daughter, and returns to the meeting. She proceeds to change a diaper on the conference table, all the while giving a brilliant advertising pitch, and she gets the job. (Hooray!) A male friend of mine said, "That scene was way over-the-top!" My response? "Been there, done that."

Survey any group of working mothers and you will hear stories just like that one—and better. Personally, I once changed my two-month-old son's blown-out diaper while moving through congested traffic in Manhattan. (Luckily, I wasn't driving.) I participated in a meeting with a group of Ivy League professors while nursing a baby. (Luckily, I wasn't driving.) These situations might sound unreal, but most working mothers know what I'm talking about. Caught in the collision between career and children, we find ourselves in hilarious situations. (At least we tell ourselves they are hilarious, because if we didn't laugh, we'd cry.)

Nell, a Yale-trained attorney, was all geared up for a big meeting. Her research, her presentation, and her appearance had been carefully prepared. Everything went as planned. All eyes were on her as she confidently walked back and forth in front of the group. Nell returned to her office in triumph, removed her suit jacket, and only then saw the perfect little handprints of her son on the back, a work of art in powdered sugar on black crepe wool. She remembered him hugging her before she left for the office, saying, "Good luck mom!"

My friend Andrea tells of the time she was running late one morning, hurrying to get her young son off to school so she would be at work on time. She got her son to school and made it into the office, then realized she was wearing two different colors of shoes.

I once forgot my youngest child at church. In all the rush I simply left him in the nursery and drove home with the other two. Thank God the nursery attendant was still there, but by the time I had realized my mistake and returned, I was hysterical. When I asked my friend Shannon what it meant to be a working mother, she said, "It means working constantly to fail at everything."

Working constantly to fail at everything. Is this the future the women's movement envisioned? Recently, as I was complaining to a group of mothers about my hectic schedule, one woman said, "The feminists made a real mess of things, making us think we could have it all." As a feminist (which I define as someone who holds the radical notion that women are people) I was shocked and a little hurt by her remark. But she's not alone. Some self-appointed cultural critics say this situation is the direct result of the women's movement. Leading the pack are people such as Dr. Laura Schlessinger, the conservative pop psychologist and professional shrew, who wrote the subtly titled book *Parenthood by Proxy: Don't Have Them If You Won't Raise Them* (Cliff Street Books, 2000). Dr. Laura and company believe that equality for women has come at the expense of our children and that we women would be happier if only we returned to our former roles as homemakers and mothers.

There are signs that some women are moving in that direction, at least temporarily. A study of Yale coeds has caused something of an uproar recently. As reported in the *New York Times*, the study revealed that 60 percent of those surveyed expect to cut back on work or stay at home after they have children.[2] Clearly, the writer seemed to suggest, this is a sign of trouble, when over half of the best and brightest are choosing to sacrifice their careers for their children. Those on the left interpret the results as a cry for help—from companies, from government, from spouses—because women would not hamstring their careers if they had adequate resources and appropriate social support systems (ignoring the possibility that some women choose motherhood *as* their career). On the right, the survey is confirmation that the next generation has wised up and has repudiated feminist values, choosing the better, more traditional life. People have begun to use the term "opt out" meaning someone (some woman) who opts out of work life in order to raise children.

Here I have to stick my socialist two cents in. Before anyone gets too far into a debate about whether or not women should stay home with their children, we ought first to consider whether or not they can. "Opting out" is a possibility for only a small part of the population—the same small part that gets admitted to places like Yale. The economic realities of modern life don't allow most women (or men) to stay at home even when they want to. Unless one spouse is making a substantial income, "opting out" is not an option. So all this talk about how bad it is to work outside the home does little to change our choices. It just makes us feel worse about them.

This feeling of inadequacy is why so many of us identify with Lynette. When Lynette "opts in" she is wracked with guilt and child care woes. In one scene Lynette, desperate to arrange in-house day care, tries to talk a stay-at-home mom into enrolling her children in the program. She pitches the day-care idea with great enthusiasm only to be rebuffed by the at-home mom, who asks matter of factly, "Why did you even have kids if you weren't going to raise them?" (Dr. Laura rides again!) Lynette responds defensively, "I'm a good mother." The woman smiles and says, "Yes, but I want to be a great mother." Ouch.

In this encounter, *Desperate Housewives* has tapped into a well of emotion and anxiety that is in all mothers, whether they work or not. This anxiety is the source of a subtle and demoralizing sort of competition that goes on between at-home mothers and working mothers, a game we play mostly in our heads to try to make ourselves feel better. Nancy, an urban planner from Minnesota, tells this story: "When I was in graduate school, I dressed casually unless I had to pick up or drop off the baby at day care. Then I would put on my 'professional' clothes so no one would mistake me for an at-home mom." When I asked her why that was important, she said, "Because there was such a stigma attached to stay-at-home mothers who put their children in day care. I wanted to make sure everyone knew I had a reason for dropping Madeline off."

I doubt that Nancy's husband ever dressed up for day-care drop-off. Even when fathers wear casual clothes, people presume that they have careers and that mothers are the primary caretakers. And while this is probably true for most families (as it is in my home) it shouldn't be the presumed norm. I still resent the fact that when there's a problem at school or day care, I get called first, even though I put my husband's name and number at the top of the emergency contact list. Last year I was sitting in a hotel lobby in Boston when my cell phone rang. It was the school secretary calling to tell me that my daughter had not been picked up after class. Trying to remain calm, I said, "I'm at a conference in Boston." The secretary replied, "So…do you want me to call your husband?"

Of course, I'm hardly one to raise the banner of equality in parenting. Somewhere in my mind is an image of "the perfect mother," a collage of cultural stereotypes and childhood memories. Super Mommy sits in my head, dressed like June Cleaver, and rattles off all the things a mother would do for her children…if only she stayed at home. Sometimes this demon of perfection overtakes my better judgment and I find myself sewing Halloween costumes at midnight on October 30 instead of buying them, or baking three-dozen cupcakes for the elementary school book fair instead of picking them up at the grocery store. This is utter folly, I know, but I think I do these things so my children won't resent me for working. The costumes and cup-cakes are just an offering to appease the working mother gods.

On the other hand, stay-at-home mothers have their own challenges and frustrations. A couple of my friends who "opted out" of outside-the-home careers to raise children feel undervalued and overworked. They tell me that in a society where you are defined by your career, "I'm a mom" isn't an acceptable answer to the question, "What do you do?" That's why some women put "domestic engineer" on forms that ask "employment?" In addition, because they don't work for pay outside of the home, everyone—from the PTA to the Scouts to the church—treats at-home mothers like an inexhaustible source of volunteer labor. One mother said, "People think that keeping a household running isn't work. But I've never worked so hard in my life!"

My friend Jennifer is always running her four children around town to activities and appointments. She's also active in her church, volunteers at the school, and has even started to work a few hours at a local hospital. Standing in the lobby of the downtown dance studio, waiting to pick up our daughters,

I asked her how she manages to do everything and remain so calm. She laughed and said, "I don't feel calm! I guess I just let go of some things. Like my house—it's a total disaster and I don't care anymore. Some day I want a beautiful house, but it will have to wait." Her comment reminded me of something my friend Nell said about being a working mother. "Any perfectionist tendencies you have disappear pretty quickly. You've got to let some things go." It would seem that modern life—whether or not you pursue a career outside the home—seems unmanageable and requires considerable compromises. At home or at work, we can't shake the feeling that we're missing something.

The problem may be the way our society values—or overvalues—work. The message is clear—you are what you do, and your status rises or falls accordingly. Consider what Edie says to Bree when she catches her having an intimate lunch with George. "Look at you! You could have an affair with anyone and you chose a pharmacist?" Clearly, George doesn't make the "A" list because of his job. (Seeing as how he turns out to be a psychotic killer, Bree probably should have stayed away from George, but not because he's a pharmacist.) Or there's poor Maisy Gibbons, who turns to prostitution to make ends meet after her husband loses his job. In an emotional speech, Maisy tells a "john" how her "friends" shunned her after she had to give up the country club membership. Maisy's career choice might strike us as strange, but at least she's keeping up appearances.

Then there's Gabrielle who is forced to look for a job after the FBI freezes the Solis's assets. In one scene, we wince as Gabrielle treats her housemaid with contempt and then fires her. But soon after, Gabrielle is working at a cosmetics counter and who should appear? Her former maid. Oh how the mighty have fallen! It's nice to see Gabrielle get a taste of her own medicine, but our appreciation of the moment is based on our understanding that working at a cosmetics counter is a demeaning occupation. Gabrielle might think she's hot stuff, but her job tells a different story.

Furthermore, it's not just what we do that determines our status, but how much we make doing it. In our society, success is generally measured in economic terms. As one ambitious man once said to me, "Money's just a way of keeping score." *Parade* magazine does an annual spread on what people make. It's nothing more than a dull list of various occupations along with the typical salary, but I can't keep myself from reading it and trying to figure out my economic value relative to others. (Last year I was somewhere between middle school teachers and dog groomers.) Every year, *Forbes* publishes a list of the highest paid CEOs. *People* magazine recently did a big spread on the richest kids in Hollywood. The message is clear—money matters. We may tell our children that "Money can't buy happiness," but the fawning attention we give to the rich tells a different story. I'm reminded of the old rock song that features this wicked line about money: "But what it can't buy, I can't use."[3]

"No one lies on their death bed and thinks, 'I should have spent more time at the office,'" goes an often-quoted maxim attributed to Paul Tsongas (though someone will undoubtedly write to tell me it was Stephen Covey or that great sage Anonymous.) In our hearts, we know that it's true. Which is why we laugh at Gabrielle. She's the embodiment of this "I want money" attitude, and we shake our heads at her undisguised greed and narcissism. Yet our economic system depends, in part, on these same values and attitudes. We may not want to be like Gabrielle, but our desire to succeed leads to the same endless striving for career advancement and monetary gain, to say nothing of long hours at the office.

Here's the trick—it turns out that the old saying is true. Money can't buy happiness. And no career, no matter how exciting or well paying, can ultimately satisfy, especially in our American economic system. Statistically speaking we're working longer hours for less pay with declining job security. Judith Warner puts it bluntly, "Work stinks for most people. Given the financial opportunity to opt out, a great many men and women alike, particularly those outside the upper middle-class, would gladly do so."[4]

I think Warner is right. Maybe the "opt out" movement isn't based on a new appreciation for the traditional role of homemaker, or the result of the sexist inequalities in our support system for working mothers. Maybe women are opting out because there is a growing realization that work is structured in a way that diminishes life for women *and* men, even those without children. As Warner concludes, "With the exception of people with extreme Type A sensibilities, 'full human flourishing' requires a certain kind of slowness in life, a certain kind of stillness, a great degree of relaxation, time for reflection and…for meaningful human connection. Those things, however, are now a luxury for most people, given the nature of life and work in our time."[5]

So how do we as Christians achieve full human flourishing? In John 10:10 Jesus says, "I came that [you] may have life, and have it abundantly." In other words, Jesus came so we might fully flourish as human beings. Jesus did not say, "I came that you might have a satisfying career," or "I came that you might make money and make it abundantly," although there are some preachers who seem to interpret him this way. From the Christian perspective, full human flourishing is not possible apart from Jesus, apart from God.

In modern secular society, our identity—our status and value—is wrapped up in what we do. It's part of human nature; we have this deep desire to create for ourselves a life and an identity such that who we are has lasting meaning and value. Yet at the end of the day the great Christian truth is that you can't make meaning in your life apart from God. In fact the attempt to justify your own life by what you do is nothing but pride, which is one definition of sin.

Meaning comes from God, and God values you. That's the beginning and end of the story, no matter who you are or what you do. Truly meaningful work—in or out of the home—is an outgrowth of the powerful conviction that God loves you. The alternative is a work life that is nothing but an ultimately futile attempt to create meaning by meeting socially constructed and constantly shifting standards of success. Now that's the definition of desperate.

CHAPTER 6

.

Sex and the Suburbs—or Dance of the Seven Tank Tops

My thirteen-year-old son asked me what chapter I was working on, and I said, "It's the one about sex." He winced, visibly, as if to say, "What's a nice mother like you doing writing about *that*?" I understand his reaction and have my own concerns about tackling such a touchy subject. But it must be done. To talk about *Desperate Housewives* without talking about sex would be like talking about Julia Child but avoiding the subject of cooking.

On Wisteria Lane, sex is everywhere and, like duct tape, used for everything. There's sex as a form of revenge, as when Carlos physically abuses Gabrielle and she runs off to have sex with John. There's sex as a method of persuasion, as when Gabrielle gives her body in exchange for what she wants. (Gabrielle and Maisy Gibbons seem to have a lot in common.) Bree uses sex as a form of marriage counseling, showing up at Rex's apartment wearing nothing but high heels, lingerie, and a

51

fur coat. Lynette's boss sleeps with the office boy as a way to make herself feel powerful. Susan approaches sex as a sort of performance, insisting that Mike come over to her place because, "I need my stuff around me." There's even sex as a source of comedy, as when Tom and Lynette discover that their mild-mannered neighbors have a penchant for homemade pornography. And Edie? Well Edie views sex the way other people view money—it's just a way of keeping score. Yes, sex has many uses on *Desperate Housewives*.

But before I get too far into the uses (and misuses) of sex on *Desperate Housewives* I need to note the abuses—and two serious abuses spring to mind. The first came in the opening montage of episode nine in the first season. It featured a series of scenes in which Gabrielle was lying on a bed (only her legs were visible) with a different man entering the room in each scene. First was her stepfather, then a fashion photographer, then Carlos on their wedding night, and then John, the teenage gardener. The camera work was very clever—the position of the men was the same, as was the sensual moving of the legs. The voice-over (angelic Mary Alice) interpreted the scenes for us, explaining how Gabrielle figured out how to use sex to get what she wants. There is no commentary, no judgment, just a revealing of events.

The problem is that what happened to the teenaged Gabrielle is sexual abuse, pure and simple. And since we are told that she and John began their affair when he was sixteen, the last scene is also a form of sexual abuse. Further confusing the matter is the sensual moving of her legs, which clearly indicates that Gabrielle is enjoying all of it, even that unwelcome first encounter. While this opening montage might provide some insight into the hypersexualized character of Gabrielle, in a society where incest and the sexual exploitation of children is a growing problem, it strikes me as a remarkably irresponsible plot device.

The second "abuse" of sex occurs at the very end of episode eight. This is the episode in which Paul Young discovers that Mrs. Huber was blackmailing his wife, which was what led Mary Alice Young to commit suicide. It's also the episode in which

Susan and Mike finally have sex. These two stories reach their climax at the same time (it's hard to talk about sex without stumbling into puns), with Paul bludgeoning Mrs. Huber with a blender at the same moment that Mike and Susan are passionately, and somewhat roughly, making love. The scenes jump between Paul and Mrs. Huber and then Mike and Susan in a way that troubled me. Watching the scene, you can't help but mix up the two stories. What are we to think? Is this just the old cliché, connecting sex and violence? Or are we supposed to equate what Paul is doing to Mrs. Huber with what Mike is doing to Susan?

What's even worse is that both stories had been moving toward this ultimate moment for weeks. I don't know about the rest of you, but I was rooting for Susan and Mike. So to see the culmination of their relationship interwoven with a bloody murder was rather sickening. We were supposed to feel happy about Susan and Mike, but were we supposed to feel similar satisfaction from the violent death of Mrs. Huber? It might have made for high ratings, but to mix sex and violence in this way shows bad judgment and very poor taste.

Clearly sex serves many functions on *Desperate Housewives*, not all of which we recognize or approve of. Most single women I spoke with expressed sympathy for Susan and her nonexistent sex life. Her search for love (and sex) strikes a cord with women who find themselves in a similar situation—trying to negotiate the world of relationships and the sexual politics that go with it. Susan knows betrayal and infidelity, so she's wary as she searches for Mr. Right (or at least Mr. Right Now). In one poignant scene, Edie takes Susan out to a bar to have a drink and maybe meet men. As they sit and drink, Susan bemoans her fate and the fate of all single women. Susan: They (men) know they have the upper hand. Edie: *We* have the upper hand! Susan: Maybe fifteen years ago, but not anymore. Now we're just lonely and desperate and they know it!

On the other hand, married women tend to identify with Lynette, whose sexual identity appears to conflict with her role as a mother. Underneath the sweat pants and baggy flannel shirts, Lynette is still sexually attractive. She and Tom obviously value their sexual relationship. But oftentimes life is just too busy and stressful. Believe it or not, there are times when sleep is more exciting than sex.

While I identify with Lynette, I don't like the way she is generally portrayed, especially when compared with the other "desperate" women. My friend Rooth shares my feelings and has decided the problem is not with Lynette, but with the show's portrayal of what is sexy and attractive.

Here's how Rooth understands the issue. The commonly held myth is that motherhood is both the most revered avocation and the most profoundly unhip and undesirable role. Mothers are asexual and selfless saints, such as June Cleaver or Edith Bunker. Therefore, in our self-centered and hypersexualized society, only a sucker would want to be a mom. Gabrielle captures this view when she explains why she's trying to hide her pregnancy from her model girlfriends. "I told them I would be rich and in love and childless, not another fat housefrau living a life I didn't plan!"

On the surface, then, it would seem that a show called *Desperate Housewives*—which features a bevy of svelte beauties—turns the old stereotype on its head. Welcome to Wisteria Lane, home of the red-hot mamas! But if you look more closely, you see that the popular myth is the dramatic engine that drives the show's machine. Rooth puts it this way, "While the pervasiveness of this 'myth' is an undeniable reality, the myth itself is not reality. To me, the drama is highly unsatisfying because it doesn't move beyond that stubborn myth, the one I stumble over everyday." I agree with Rooth. Being a mother does not mean you've given up being sensual or sexy. But don't tell that to the writers of *Desperate Housewives*.

To see how the myth of the unsexy mom is reinforced, simply line up the women according to "magnitude of motherhood." Scoring a zero on the motherhood scale is Edie, the blond bombshell. (She seems to have once had a son, but he disappeared in the pilot—talk about a bad mother!) She's so sexy even the construction workers are rendered mute. A classic Edie moment occurs during the fashion show when Edie arrives in a short, short dress. "Can you tell I'm not wearing any underwear?" she asks. "Yes!" the others reply. "Good!" says Edie.

Competing with Edie for the title of sex kitten is Gabrielle. Gabby is furious when she finds out she's pregnant (Carlos sabotages her birth control pills). Her concern is for her image and her figure, and children simply don't fit in the picture. Anyone with an ounce of sense could tell that Gabrielle would eventually lose the baby, because Gabrielle's primary *modus operandi* is sex, and in the world according to *Desperate Housewives,* sex and motherhood don't mix.

Then there's Susan, who seems to have become a mother by mistake. One episode opens with a series of flashbacks in which we see how incompetent a mother Susan has always been. She leaves baby Julie unattended on a couch, spills food on her, and even forgets her in the apartment. As mentioned earlier, Susan is one of those nontraditional, best-friend kinds of mothers. Which is probably why Susan is allowed to be sexy, though often in a comical and exaggerated way.

Bree and Lynette, whose primary identities are as mothers, are as far from sexy as you can get. Bree is the cold saint, sort of a Vulcan version of Harriet Nelson. Rex and Bree, we are to presume, have a dull and conventional sex life, that is, until Rex talks Bree into taking a walk on the wild side with a little S&M. But don't mistake Bree's willingness to dominate Rex as a sign that she is warming to the idea. The first time Rex broaches the subject, he does so by producing a pair of handcuffs. Bree looks at the cuffs and finally says, "Do you mind if I run these through the dishwasher first?"

Whereas Bree is the model of bloodless—and sexless—perfection, Lynette is a mother on the edge of a nervous breakdown. Taking care of the house and her four children leaves Lynette little time to care for herself. As a result, Lynette usually looks like she just crawled out of bed. In one funny scene, Tom and Lynette start to make love, but when Tom gets close to her, he recoils at a foul smell. "Oh, that's where the baby spit up," she explains. "It kind of soaked in." Far from sexy, motherhood actually stinks in this depiction.

Worse yet, when the moms try to be sexy, they make fools of themselves. Lynette, desperate to put some spark back in her marriage, dresses up in a ridiculous French maid outfit. But by the time Tom comes home, Lynette has fallen asleep ungracefully on the couch, and when she startles awake, she is embarrassed to find that Tom has brought home a coworker to spend the night in the guest bedroom. Cue the laugh track. And remember Bree's attempting to win Rex back by showing up at his apartment in little more than a fur coat and heels? Rex is, of course, delighted by the surprise, but when the couple is in bed, Bree becomes obsessed with a half-eaten burrito about to spill its gooey contents on the nightstand, and the mood is broken. Bree is such a mom that she can't stop cleaning even in the midst of a clinch.

Still think I might be overstating the case? Take a look around at the women who are shown at the park, running the PTA meetings, and escorting their children to birthday parties—it's a lumpy sea of smocks, turtlenecks and theme sweaters. It reminds me of the recent commercial send-up on *Saturday Night Live* for "Mom Jeans," in which the usually sharp, svelte *SNL* women are seen dressed in loose, unfashionable clothing, with their tummies, hips and butts amply padded. Sporting outdated haircuts and little makeup, the "moms" awkwardly frolic around while the jingle music plays: "Mom Jeans! For when you've given up giving it up!" ("Giving it up" being popular slang for being sexy, having sex, and attracting male attention.) *Desperate Housewives* isn't quite so obvious (or funny) as *SNL*, but the show sings the same song—married women with children aren't sexy.

The stereotype of the sexless mother is so deeply ingrained in our culture that it has generated its own forbidden fruit. In 2005 one of the most popular songs on the radio was "Stacy's Mom" by Fountains of Wayne. Against a catchy rock-and-roll beat, the lead singer croons in the voice of teenage boy who has fallen for his friend's mother. "Stacy's mom has got it goin' on!" And recently I learned that there are dozens of pornographic Web sites labeled "MILF," which stands for "mothers I'd like to…" This is not progress. Whether mothers are portrayed as sexless objects or as sex objects, being objects at all still means we are not allowed to be fully human.

So if mothers aren't sexy, then neither is marriage. This is another myth that *Desperate Housewives* exploits—married people have lousy sex lives. It's like the old joke—Ole and Lena are watching TV, and Ole says, "Whatever happened to our sexual relations?" After a moment, Lena responds, "I don't know. I don't think we even got a Christmas card from them this year." Our laughter depends on the common cultural assumption that marriage and sexual fulfillment are mutually exclusive. Look around Wisteria Lane: the really steamy sex is illicit, while the married sex is…uninspiring. My sister Kaia, after seeing just one episode, asked, "So what's up with Tom and Lynette? Their relationship is completely sexless. I thought this was supposed to be some sort of sexy show?"

I understand my sister's confusion. *Desperate Housewives* is a very sexy and sensual show. The whole setting—from the manicured nails to the manicured lawns—is a hypersensualized extension of the body. Pay attention to the baths, the food, the lingerie, the candles, and the clothing. There's nothing on Wisteria Lane to distract from the banquet of sensuality; the flotsam and jetsam of real life has been hidden away so as not to "spoil the mood." As a friend of mine wondered, "Where's the garbage? Where are the dirty dishes, the old leftovers, the abandoned lunches, the unfolded laundry? Do they even have bathrooms?" Of course they have bathrooms—where else are the women going to take those long, hot baths?

Yes, it's a sensual and sexy place where the "Desperate Housewives" dwell. But for all the overt eroticism, there's remarkably little going on. In other words, sex is everywhere *and* nowhere. It's the ultimate big tease. Consider a typical scene:

Gabrielle finally has a conjugal visit with Carlos in prison, and she throws her clothes off to reveal yet another Victoria's Secret lingerie set. The couple falls into bed and...break for a commercial. I'm reminded of those Barbara Cartland bodice rippers we used to read as kids. "The swarthy Viking prince pulled Juliet close to him, so close she could feel his manhood. She tilted her head up to kiss her beloved captor and...Chapter 3." The chapter would always end before there was a satisfactory explanation of the ellipses.

In the same fashion, returning from the commercial break, we find Gabriel and Carlos just finishing up (as it were) but wait! She's still wearing her lingerie! What's going on here? Is Gabrielle too shy to disrobe? It's been years since *NYPD Blue* gave us a shot of reality—and a shot of David Caruso's average naked tush—so why does *Desperate Housewives* keep the lid on? It's a dance of the seven tank tops that ultimately reveals nothing of worth.

Now some people might argue that because *Desperate Housewives* is broadcast in the early part of prime time, the writers and producers don't have the freedom to portray sexual intimacy in realistic terms. After all, there might be children watching. But any child who's seen Mary Alice blow her brains out against the wall or watched Paul beat Mrs. Huber to death with a blender can probably handle a little physical intimacy between married adults. Certainly the time slot does not explain this situational prudishness. Instead, I think the "all sizzle and no steak" of *Desperate Housewives* is simply a reflection of our culture's fundamental discomfort with human sexuality.

We live in a culture that, like *Desperate Housewives,* is awash in sexuality. Advertisers use sex to sell everything from clothes to liquor to cars. ("What's under your hood?" purrs a current ad for trucks.) Sex seems to be the only viable topic for popular music. (One of my favorite groups, The Black Eyed Peas, recently released a simply hideous song entitled "My Humps," featuring perhaps the worst lyrics since Captain and Tennille sang of "Muskrat Love.") The current trends in youth fashion seem designed to make all young women look like Jodie Foster playing the teen hooker in *Taxi Driver.* (Fashions have become so revealing that the local middle school sent home a letter at the start of the fall semester explaining what constituted "appropriate attire" for girls. Apparently, bare bellies and visible thongs are distracting to adolescent boys. Who knew?) And pornography has been transformed from a taboo subject relegated to the sleazy backrooms of adult bookstores into a billion-dollar industry that has its own trade shows and unions.

American popular culture is obsessed with sex, but only in a very limited sense. Sex is great, but human sexuality—now there's a taboo subject. We like sexy entertainment but only if it's disconnected from embodied reality. Once you start dealing with human sexuality as a whole—including relationships, intimacy, practices, and reproduction—the average person changes the channel.

This disjointed approach to human sexuality is reflected in the stories on *Desperate Housewives.* Sure, we see Susan preparing her bedroom for the special "first time" with Mike, but there's no sign anyone is worrying about birth control. We're led to believe that Edie has slept with just about every man who's stumbled onto Wisteria Lane, but does she ever worry about sexually transmitted diseases? No way! Bree's son, Andrew, is sleeping with another young man, but there's no discussion of safe sex, just a display of homophobia on Bree's part. And the subject of abstinence is used as a source of comedy, not thoughtful discussion or even real drama.

I think this obsession with sex but discomfort with human sexuality sends a confusing message to our children, a message that comes from both sides of the political spectrum. On the right, the operating assumption seems to be that if you teach children about human sexuality, they will become sexually active. Which reminds me of the *Desperate Housewives* episode in which Bree discovers a condom in the laundry and comes to the conclusion it belongs to Andrew. She tells Rex that she isn't going to give the condom back to Andrew because "he'll be tempted to use it." Rex speaks the truth when he responds, "Bree, he's a teenage boy. You could take away his penis, and he'd still try to have sex." We're just fooling ourselves if we think "abstinence only" education is adequate to the task of teaching our children how to deal with their own powerful sexuality. In other words, to say "just don't do it" is useless without a thoughtful and thorough discussion of what "it" is. How else do we explain the fact that the rates of sexually transmitted diseases are the same among high school students who have signed abstinence pledges and those who have not? Sure, we told them to abstain, but we were too embarrassed to tell them from what—or why.

The liberal alternative seems to be an "owner's manual" approach to human sexuality, one that emphasizes the mechanics without regard to the morality. Perhaps we presume that parents will tackle that part of this touchy subject. Unfortunately there's little evidence to suggest parents are up to the task. My friend Andrea summarizes the sex education she got in her Baptist home in one sentence, "Keep your skirt down!" On the other end of the spectrum, when I excitedly told my parents of my first chaste kiss at age thirteen, I received a long and carefully prepared lecture on sexuality and human relationships, which I later comically summarized for my friends as the "kissing leads to marriage" talk. Parents aside, the attitude on the left seems to be, "They're going to do it anyway. We might as well show them how it's done safely."

Neither of these approaches treats human sexuality as a whole, addressing the physical, spiritual, emotional, and moral implications. The former turns sex into a mysterious and forbidden thing, best handled through an unquestioning and unthinking adherence to rules. The latter turns sex into just another physical activity divorced from meaning and emotion. Yet I think the reason we don't know how to address human sexuality with our children is because we don't know how we feel about it ourselves.

Our problems began back in Eden. Genesis 1:26–31 gives us a wonderful account of the creation of humans. "So God created humankind in his image, in the image of God he created them; male and female he created them. God blessed them, and God said to them, 'Be fruitful and multiply.'" (Gen. 1:27–28a) At the end of the process, God looked upon everything that had been made, "and indeed, it was very good." (Gen. 1:31) Then there was all that trouble with the serpent and the forbidden fruit, and Adam and Eve ate from the tree of knowledge, and suddenly they saw themselves, not as God saw them, but through their own sinful eyes. "Yikes! We're naked!" and on go the fig leaves, and suddenly the body becomes something to be ashamed of. And sex, which is so grounded in the physical, gets a bad reputation by association.

What we need to remember is that sex is not, in and of itself, a sin. From the very beginning, human sexuality—in all its miraculous and messy complexity—has been a gift from God. But like all gifts, sex and sexuality can be misused or even abused. And while there's no exact biblical prescription for a healthy sexual relationship, we do know that Jesus calls us to relationships that are loving, faithful, committed, and monogamous. (I don't believe such relationships are confined to marriage, because only heterosexuals are able to legally marry. I've known dozens of same-sex couples who embody these Christian values.) It is within the boundaries of such Christian love that God's good gift of human sexuality can be received and enjoyed to the fullest extent. That's why married sex is the best sex—it is the physical expression of an inward unity of hearts. (Plus, remember what your teachers always said, "Practice makes perfect.") Outside of this context, sex loses its integrity and becomes, to quote Gabrielle, "just sex."

I was eight years old when I first saw *The Ten Commandments* in all its Technicolor glory, and the scene the made the biggest impression on me was when Aaron and the Hebrews made the golden calf. It's such a Cecil B. DeMille moment, with men and women frolicking around this shiny giant cow. People were dancing and drinking and chasing around. Among the throng, one group captured my attention: a woman was laughing and running away from a group of men who finally caught her. They raised her up over their heads and carried her writhing body off screen and…(break for a commercial?) At the time I had no idea what was happening or what was going to happen, but I knew that even though it seemed like fun and games, something was very wrong.

An idol is something you worship above all other things, the object of your heart's desire. Truth is, we are gifted idol makers, capable of turning almost anything into our own personal golden calf. When we treat sex as just a physical act, a source of personal pleasure rather than a gift from God to be given to our beloved, it becomes a form of idolatry and we've fallen into sin—just as some of the folks on Wisteria Lane have done.

There's a final point to make, and it may be the most important. Part of our squeamishness around this subject stems from our general discomfort with our own bodies. Bodies are such messy, bothersome things, prone to breaking down and subject to the ravages of time and gravity. When it comes to bodies, we'd prefer to keep everything under wraps, figuratively and literally. But we can't.

Popular culture screams at us that the only really good bodies are young and beautiful, perfectly shaped and ripe with sexuality. This is a standard none of us can achieve in real life. As our bodies age and change, we begin to despise them, hide them, disguise them cosmetically and even surgically, which means, of course, we begin to despise ourselves. When we are ashamed of our real bodies, we begin to be ashamed of our true selves.

Part of what Christians mean by the incarnation is that we value real bodies. For Christians, God is not an idea or an untouchable enigma. God "became flesh and lived among us" (Jn. 1:14). Jesus didn't float down from heaven. He was born to a mother who suffered through labor, just like other human beings. Jesus himself had a body, not a glossy, make-believe body, but a real body that grew hungry and tired, a body that bled when he was wounded.

We believe that the incarnation, God coming to us in true human form, is very good news. It means that our bodies are not shameful, but sacred. Our real bodies, the very ones that age and change and finally die, are not a source of embarrassment, but temples of the Holy Spirit. Therefore, everything we do with our bodies—including making love—is potentially an act of holiness. To come to grips with the incarnation is also to grapple with what it means to be embodied, creatures of flesh and bone. Incarnation is about bodies and blood and water and food—and all the messy stuff of life—that through the incarnation becomes the stuff of love. "This is my body, which is given for you" (Lk. 22.19). Through Jesus, we—body and soul—are made whole and holy.

CHAPTER 7

With Friends Like These...

Here's the scene. Gabrielle and Carlos are broke and go to outrageous lengths to hide their financial problems. Finally, Bree begins to suspect something is amiss. She broaches the subject with Gabrielle, saying, "If you and Carlos are having financial trouble, you should have asked for help. That's what friends are for." Gabrielle denies they are having trouble and then pointedly asks Bree where Andrew has been. (He's been sent off to a camp for delinquent youth.) There's a tense pause, then Gabrielle says, "Good friends avoid each other after they've been humiliated. Great friends pretend nothing happened in the first place."

Gabrielle's definition of friendship reminds me of something my cousin once said to me. "A good friend will help you move. A great friend will help you move a body." Both definitions are facetious, of course, but somehow Gabrielle's words made me wince. Her comment seemed to diminish the quality of the relationships on Wisteria Lane.

If you've only watched an episode or two of *Desperate House-wives*, it might be hard to believe these women are friends. What could possibly have brought them together? Was it their shared love of revealing clothing? Did they all show up at a meeting of the local Manolo Blahnik fan club? Given their beautiful manes, perhaps they share the same colorist. It certainly wasn't a Junior League event—there's not a lot of civic engagement among these women. The world may never know what forged the bonds that hold the housewives together. The pilot episode simply introduces us to these four friends and leaves it at that.

My sister watched a couple episodes and remarked, "If I had friends like these, I'd shoot myself too." But if you watch the show over time, the relationships begin to take shape. These are not just neighbors; these are good friends. They bring food to the funerals, watch one another's children, and attend the weekly poker games. Despite all the plot machinations and implausible mysteries, Bree, Lynette, Susan and Gabrielle stick together.

These female friendships are the most realistic aspect of the show, even when the circumstances are extreme. When Mike dumps Susan and she runs into the street (wearing, by sad coincidence, her mother's wedding dress), the other three come out of their homes to comfort her. When Rex has his second heart attack (because George, the homicidal pharmacist, has tampered with his medication), the other women show up at the hospital in various states of dress in the middle of the night in order to support Bree. When Bree spanks Lynette's ill-behaved son (Mother Teresa would have done the same), Lynette and Bree have a falling out and stop talking to each other. Eventually Lynette walks across the street to apologize. But before Lynette says a word, Bree says, "You don't have to say anything. The fact that you crossed that street means a lot to me." Regular viewers can tell—these women may be desperate, but they are true friends.

Friendship has a high value on *Desperate Housewives*. Edie has no female friends, as one opening scene explains, and she suspects she's missing something. So when Martha Huber befriends Edie (in Martha's own judgmental way), Edie is plainly delighted. It's not the sort of friendship any of us would care to have, but for Edie, it's better than nothing. (And who else is going to tell her she's dressed like a tramp?)

Ask any woman about the importance of her friends and you're likely to get an enthusiastic response. "I'd be lost without my friends," said one woman in my church. My friend Andrea admitted, "my girlfriends keep me sane." I often think my husband should send my friends money occasionally, because they save him from having to listen to me 24/7, like some Shawnthea version of CNN: All Shawnthea, all the time. Speaking for myself—and for most of the women I know—friends are an essential part of life. They keep me connected, hold me accountable, offer comfort and encouragement, and give me great joy.

One of the ways friends keep us connected is by tying us to the past. Miriam has known me since second grade, though she would be quick to point out that she thought I was very bossy back then. In high school we became best friends, and that friendship has survived (and thrived) through our six college degrees, two husbands, five children, and multiple moves. Miriam and I talk in the rapid fire staccato of two people who have known each other all of their adult lives. No need to speak in full sentences, we have a sort of shorthand that makes for more efficient conversation. (Just say the words "country house," and we start laughing.) Ours was an ideal adolescent friendship. I taught Miriam how to meet guys; she taught me the meaning of Christian forgiveness. Even as our lives have taken us in different directions, we cherish this relationship. She is the surest connection to my youth and to the dreams of youth. With Miriam, our shared history grounds me and gives me a sense of where I've come from.

Friends also connect us to the present and even help us deal with reality. Ready to slap your children? Call a friend. Think your husband's having an affair? Time for coffee. Depressed that you can't fit into a favorite pair of pants? Talk to someone who's been there, worn that. Once, when I was furious with my husband, my sister-in-law Nancy listened to me air my petty complaints and then said, "You want me to hold him while you hit him?" (My husband certainly owes her money.) Whether you are working at home or the office; living in the country, city or suburb; married or single; friends make a difference. Why else do you think Mrs. McCluskey clings to Lynette? And why else do we cheer when Lynette makes an effort to befriend her?

A circle of friends can be especially important for women who are moving into nontraditional fields. When I was serving my first church, I signed up for a denominationally sponsored "colleague group," which was advertised as "a long-term gathering of mutually supportive colleagues" (a.k.a. friends). The group consisted of five women and one dour man, and we were scheduled to meet monthly for two years. The women immediately formed a close bond of friendship, sharing their joys and frustrations with ministry, encouraging one another through church fights and personal battles. At one of the last meetings the lone man attended, we started discussing the sexism we encounter in ministry. It's a real problem, but he was very unsympathetic. Soon after that our group was down to five, and we met for four years.

Yet there's more to friendship than connection; friends hold us accountable. There's a saying, "Only your friends can tell you the truth". That is true. Who else can get close enough to give me a word of correction? And who else would I trust to have my best interests in mind? You see this on *Desperate Housewives* when Susan discovers Gabrielle is having an affair with John. Susan confronts Gabrielle, who justifies her adultery, saying, "It's just sex! It's harmless!" Susan responds bitterly, "It's not harmless! You remember what I was like when I found out about Carl's affair! It's not harmless!" Mama Solis probably felt the same way, but Gabrielle would only take the hard truth from a friend. (Of course, Gabrielle continues to have the affair, so my point should probably be: Only friends can tell us the truth, and only friends still love us when we ignore it.)

Friends also hold us accountable to our true selves. This is a little harder to understand, but here is one way it works. I have found over the years that one of the most useful questions to ask couples before they marry is, "Do you get along with your fiancé's friends?" If the answer is no, something is amiss. Generally, people have known their friends longer than they've known their future spouse, and if those folks who know us best dislike our choice of mate, we might have chosen the wrong mate.

Years ago, my husband and I invited a friend and her new fiancé over for dinner. Within ten minutes we hated this guy. Sure, he was cute, but he was also pompous, self-centered, and stupid (I'm sure his transcript would prove my point.) Every time he joined in the conversation, he steered it toward himself without any regard for the rest of us. By the end of the meal, Neil and I were exchanging desperate looks across the table. I had made a cake, but the thought of coffee and dessert with this guy was more than I could bear. Suddenly, Neil looked at his watch and said, "Gosh! If we're going to make that movie, we'd better get going." Picking up on his cue, I stood up and said, "Oh, is it that late? I'll get my coat." We literally pushed the couple out the door (the party was at our house), got into our car, and drove around the block. We sat in the dark, laughing, waiting for them to drive away.

Turns out none of her friends liked this guy. We tried a few times to tell her how we felt, but it seemed like meddling. The marriage lasted only six years, during which time I rarely saw my girlfriend. But when it ended, we all gathered around her in support. As she poured out her tale of woe ("He's so self-centered! He never thinks of anyone but himself!"), we nodded. And finally one of us said sheepishly, "None of us ever liked him." "So why didn't you tell me? That's what friends are for!" Yes, that's what friends are for. They hold us accountable to our true selves.

Another way to look at it came from my friend Andrea. Her therapist asked her, "How do you come to your self-soothing?" Her response? "It's my faith and my friends. I have a great community of people who love and understand me, who know who I am even when I don't know myself." When we forget who we are or what is important, our true friends remind us of what's really important.

There is also a kind of comfort that only close friends can bring. When Miriam had her second child, she fell into a deep postpartum depression. I tried to cheer her up over the phone, listening to her worries and fears, trying to reduce her anxiety to normal levels, encouraging her to get medical help. But nothing worked. So I packed up my daughter, and the two of us went to St. Louis for a visit. Our daughters played together while Miriam and I talked and played with the new baby. I even watched all the children so Miriam and her husband could go out for lunch. There was nothing heroic in my actions, but the visit (plus time and good antidepressants) made a difference.

Later the next year, my mother-in-law ended up living in my house for two weeks while she recovered from back surgery. It was a stressful time for all of us, but particularly hard on me as I struggled to keep up the illusion that I kept a perfect house (see chapter 4). More than once I called Miriam in tears, overwhelmed with all the responsibilities I had to shoulder, most of which I had put on myself. Not long after, I got a letter in the mail from a local day spa. It was a gift certificate for "the full treatment," to be scheduled at my convenience. And it was from Miriam. Good friends know what you need, when you need it—and they find a way to get it to you.

Friends walk with us down every road, no matter how difficult or long the journey. I have seen friends go through the worst of times—the death of a mother, the end of a marriage, the loss of a baby—when words and actions fail, and I have nothing to offer but my presence. But presence is what really matters in those moments.

At this point, I feel the need to get up on a small but important soapbox and speak passionately on the subject of condolence cards. Death is such a stranger in this culture. It's hidden away as if there were something unnatural or embarrassing about it. To further complicate matters, we've become a post-Christian society where fewer and fewer people are familiar with the rites and language of faith. So when someone dies, it has the effect of rendering us speechless and at the same time demanding that we say something. We want to be supportive, but no one knows how to respond. So we send a sympathy card with a well-chosen verse or smattering of scripture, maybe enclose a memorial gift and sign it: With deepest sympathy. Maybe it's just me, but such cards seem like cold comfort. No one remembers the exact cards they received. What they remember are the words, written in an unsure hand, which expressed love and sorrow and even helplessness. So don't just sign the sympathy card; write a few words. Better yet, send a letter with a few memories, an expression of sorrow, and a promise to stay in touch. Presence is what really matters.

Back to friendship: a woman from my church said this about friends, "They double your joy and halve your sorrow." I think it's true. Just as they bring comfort in times of distress, no one can celebrate your triumphs like your friends because they know exactly what it took to succeed.

A sensitive reader will notice that this chapter suffers from serious gender bias, speaking about friendship as if it were only a female phenomenon. This is probably because male friendships are a mystery to me, seeming to consist of televised sports, amateur athletic competitions, and office politics. Actually, this flippant response is based in some truth. Men form strong friendships over shared activities, without necessarily spending a lot of time talking. If you ask my husband who his best friend is, he'll probably tell you it's Paul, whom he has spoken to exactly twice in the last year. I have spoken to my best friend twice...in the last twenty-four hours. I have no doubt that men form similarly close albeit quieter attachments, but male and female friendships are very different. Perhaps someone will explore this subject in a later book: *Monday (Night Football) with Morrie.*

While we are talking about issues of gender, it seems like the right time to discuss one of the threats to female relationships—competition. Like it or not, women have a strong desire to gain masculine approval. In other words, we compete for the attention of men. Recall the episode where Lynette's female boss keeps dragging her out to bars after work. Her boss doesn't care that Lynette has children and a husband at home, so Lynette fights fire with fire. She strips down to a vest and pants, and dances on the bar while all the men cheer, much to the dismay of her boss. And—surprise!—her boss never invites Lynette out to a bar again.

Why do we behave like this? Some suggest it's the result of evolutionary hardwiring. In the struggle to pass on our genetic material, women figured out that gaining male approval was the key to survival. Others suggest it's the lingering and pernicious effects of sexism. Practically from the moment we emerge from the womb, women are bombarded with the message that it is good to be attractive to men. I don't know which theory I find more persuasive. All I know is that at the age of two, my daughter would stand at the screen door and call out to the twelve-year-old neighbor boy, "Hi Zach! Hi! Hi Zach!" her voice taking on an unmistakable lilt.

This competition for male attention can drive us to extremes. On *Desperate Housewives* it causes Susan to burn down Edie's house. (It *was* an accident.) Elsewhere on television, it leads to noxious programs such as *The Bachelor*, on which a collection of otherwise talented and sensible women put themselves in humiliating situations, all to get the attention of one man. (I keep waiting for one of the girls to sneer, "Is that a rose in your pocket or are you just glad to see me?") In real life, it leads to a 700 percent jump in cosmetic surgeries in the last ten years.

There's nothing new about this vying for male approval. One of the formative stories in the Old Testament is the story of Rachel and Leah (Gen. 29:1—30:24). Recall the facts: Jacob, fleeing his brother's wrath, runs into Rachel, daughter of Laban, and instantly falls in love with her. He agrees to work seven years for Laban in exchange for Rachel's hand. But on the wedding night, Laban slips the ugly older sister (Leah, whose eyes were weak) into the tent, and Jacob ends up consummating a marriage to the wrong woman. (Was it really that dark?) The next morning, Laban and Jacob strike another bargain, and after seven more years, Jacob finally gets the object of his desire, Rachel.

The two sisters—the beloved and the other—engage in a desperate competition for Jacob's affection based on who can produce the most male children, sort of a womb versus womb battle for the boy. Eager to win, the women even offer their maids as surrogates until Jacob is the father of twelve sons (and at least one daughter), who become the twelve tribes of Israel. Thus, woven into the very history of Judaism is this female striving for male attention.

This competition is not simply expressed in physical or sexual terms. As my friend Shannon quipped, "I'm smarter than I am pretty, so I compete professionally." That would explain why women who move up the corporate ladder tend not to bring other women with them—we simply can't stand the competition. Perhaps that also explains why the group most likely to give a female pastor a hard time is other women her age.

The seeking of masculine approval—whether it's on *Desperate Housewives* or in the real world—shapes and distorts our friendships and even our identities. Imagine what Edie would look like if her sense of well-being didn't depend on male approval! Imagine what Susan would be like if she was happily single. Imagine what Gabrielle could do with her time if she could see herself through her own eyes, rather than the eyes of men. (OK, so it would be a really boring show, but you get my point.)

A single-sex environment can be very valuable. In college, I lived in the only single-sex dorm at the University of Minnesota, Comstock Hall (known alternatively as the Virgin Vault and Livestock Hall). Every year, some group of women would circulate a petition to make Comstock co-ed, like the other dorms on campus. And every year, the petition would be overwhelmingly rejected. One night in the dining room, I asked another resident why she voted against the change. Her reply? "Who wants to be 'on' for breakfast? I'd like to have at least one place I don't have to wear makeup all the time." The presence of men shapes how women perceive themselves and how they act.

Let me be clear. I'm not blaming men or women for this state of affairs. In my opinion, it's just another sign of the fall, another facet of this flawed and broken world. But if we could see ourselves and other people in a new way—through the eyes of God—I think we'd discover unimagined and holy possibilities in friendship.

The story of Ruth and Naomi (from the book of Ruth) is a marvelous tale of the holy possibilities of friendship. After the deaths of her husband and sons, Naomi has no economic resources. She must return to her homeland and try to find a way to survive. Her daughter-in-law Orpah decides to remain in Moab, but the other daughter-in-law, Ruth, begs to stay with Naomi. Ruth's touching words to Naomi are a powerful expression of devotion:

> "Do not press me to leave you
>   or to turn back from following you!
> Where you go, I will go;
>   where you lodge, I will lodge;
> your people shall be my people,
>   and your God, my God.
> Where you die, I will die—
>   there will I be buried.
> May the LORD do thus and so to me,
>   and more as well,
> if even death parts me from you!" (Ruth 1:16–17)

There's no social contract between Ruth and Naomi—only the bonds of friendship, love, and trust, which transcend the structures of society and culture. And together, they find a way not only to survive but to thrive, a way that eventually leads to the birth of David. Thus friendship, in the Jewish tradition, lays the foundation for the kingdom of David. But friendship, in the Christian tradition, lays the foundation for the kingdom of God.

As he prepares to go to the cross, Jesus gives his disciples a new identity. "This is my commandment, that you love one another as I have loved you. No one has greater love than this, to lay down one's life for one's friends. You are my friends if you do what I command you" (Jn. 15:12–14). To be friends, in the Christian sense of the word, is to love selflessly and completely, without envy, bitterness, or competition. A friend is someone who, like Jesus, can wholeheartedly revel in the success of another, someone who wants to see you flourish. In this way friendship is the smallest unit of Christian community and Christian identity, the place where grace hits the ground.

My friend Andrea puts it another way, "My friends are a tangible version of what I get from God—unconditional love and acceptance—and they give living proof to what Jesus is all about, reassuring me that I am not alone."

In the context of true Christian friendship, we can be fully ourselves and fully open to the reality of the other person. There is something profoundly moving about this knowing of another, which is why Jesus says, "I do not call you servants any longer, because the servant does not know what the master is doing; but I have called you friends, because I have made known to you everything that I have heard from my Father" (Jn. 15:15).

How would our world change if we could see every person—from the TV star to the homeless man—as a friend? What would our friendships look like if we could truly support one another? How would we treat one another if we had a deeper appreciation for real friendship?

Let's return to the friendships on *Desperate Housewives*. After Gabrielle and Carlos have almost come to the end of their financial rope, Bree returns for a visit. Sitting on the porch with Gabrielle, she hands her an envelope and says, "Rex and I have decided not to renew our country club membership. And I thought the money could be put to better use." Gabrielle looks inside, and tears well up in her eyes. She starts to say something about paying it back, but Bree says, "Take your time. Good friends offer to help in a crisis. Great friends don't take no for an answer." Now that's friendship.

CHAPTER 8

As You Have Done to the Least of These

I wasn't much of a *Star Trek* fan, but I can still remember one scary episode. It involved a planet that had been decimated by a disease that struck anyone over the age of thirty, causing childlike behavior, dementia, and finally death. At first the crew thinks all is well, but then someone (I think it was Lt. Uhura) has a sudden realization. "Captain! They're all children. Where are the old people?" (Cue ominous music!)

I had the opposite experience visiting my parents in Sun City West. At first, everything seemed fine, but then I started to notice there were no playgrounds, no public schools, no strollers choking the grocery store aisles. Then I had a sudden realization. "Captain! They're all old people. Where are the children?" (Cue the laugh track.) These are both examples of the background becoming the foreground.

Life is like a play, with a background and a foreground. The background is the accidental setting against which the action takes place. We tend not to notice it. The foreground is where the action is, whatever is engaging our attention and focus. Sometimes we notice something in the background that hadn't caught our attention previously. ("Captain! Where are the old people?") But it usually has to be way out of whack before we notice it, because we're focused on the business at hand. In other words, the foreground is the cup of coffee I am drinking. The background is the cup of coffee someone at another table is drinking. But if that woman drops her cup of coffee, the background becomes the foreground. All clear?

Although it doesn't get much focus, the background has a lot of power. We passively take in information about the world from the background. For example, if you've only seen doctors who are male, you might come to believe that only men can be doctors. This is the same reason there is a push to get men into elementary education. I learned this lesson some years ago when I was out of town for two weeks and two retired men filled the pulpit in my absence. I asked my son how he liked church. He said, "It was ok. But I just can't get used to seeing a guy up there." Ah yes. Changing the background can make a real difference. And sometimes it's not what is being said, but who is saying it that matters.

On television, nothing is accidental. Even the background is freighted with meaning. Take a look around Wisteria Lane. Pay attention to the size and color of the houses, the placement of the flowers, the kinds of cars parked on the street, even the weather. Every element of the background has been designed to send a specific message—this is the good life. It looks like the garden of Eden, or the American version of suburban paradise, or a Jehovah's Witness tract come to life. Watching *Desperate Housewives,* we passively take in the show's version of the perfect world, focusing all our attention on the trials and tribulations of the housewives.

But wait. You have a sudden realization, "Captain! They're all white, able-bodied rich people! Where is *everyone else?*" Wisteria Lane seems to have been zoned "minority free." Of course you might point out that many shows make similar artistic choices. Where are the African Americans on *Will & Grace?* Where are the poor on *Dallas?* But *Desperate Housewives* pretends to be a typical community. And while relatively few of us will ever be single and gay in NYC, or wealthy oil barons on some oversized ranch in Texas, many of us live—or hope to live—in a suburban community.

In truth, there are a few minority characters on *Desperate Housewives,* but that's almost more troubling. Either they are portrayed in an unthinking and unsympathetic manner (why is the murderous private detective African American?) or they are used for strange dramatic effect (what's really wrong with Betty Applewhite's son?). As a Christian, I think we need to bring this background into the foreground as a way of understanding what message *Desperate Housewives* is broadcasting when it comes to minorities. After all, Jesus tells us, "As you have done to the least of these, so you have done to me" (Mt. 25:40)

Betty Applewhite was a late addition to the Wisteria Lane cast. She and her son snuck into town under cover of darkness, clearly hiding their own terrible secrets. But it was a splash of diversity in an otherwise white (or off-white) cast. When I mentioned to an African American friend, Andrea, that Wisteria Lane had been integrated, she responded, "Yes, it's great. The black woman's a criminal, the Hispanic woman's amoral—I think it's setting us back."

She has a point. Start keeping track of the people of color *on Desperate Housewives* and you'll soon spot a disturbing trend. Most of the African Americans are shady characters. There's the detective who nearly kills Edie; Caleb Applewhite, who may or may not have attacked a young girl; and Caleb's family, who seem to live by the motto that justice, like charity, begins at home. Betty is shown slapping her eldest son and threatening her younger son, sometimes with a gun. And when Carlos and Gabrielle are sitting in the couple's counseling session in prison, the camera pans around the circle, showing that nearly everyone is black. This may or may not be an accurate representation of the current prison population,[1] but it seems odd for the writers to have moved into cinema verité for this one scene.

Then we find the grouchy Asian housekeeper, who relishes Gabrielle's downfall behind the cosmetics counter, and the unseen evil Asian businessman, Mr. Tanaka, who is making money off of slave labor and feeling up Gabrielle at parties. And there is the Solis family, who seem to have been pulled off a shelf at central casting, the one labeled "red hot Hispanics."

Carlos is all posturing machismo, with a stereotypical temper and taste for fitted suits. He may have money, but he lacks good taste, instead purchasing things that are gaudy, flashy, and expensive. (Remember that hand-carved table Gabrielle and John had sex on during the first episode?) He worships his mother, has an unthinking faith in the Catholic Church, and will revert to his basest instincts when pushed.

Mama Solis, looking petty and pudgy, appears to have wandered out of a spaghetti western, setting aside her mantilla as she walks in the door. She loves her son to the exclusion of all other people and will do anything to make her daughter-in-law look bad. (I could spend a whole chapter on the way *Desperate Housewives* treats mothers-in-law, but space forbids.)

Gabrielle is the red-hot Hispanic girl who values nothing but shopping, money, and sex. We are led to believe that Edie is the resident slut, but in the first episode we learn that Gabrielle has slept with half the outfield of the Mets. Even though she seems about as Hispanic as Taco Bell, Gabrielle is the only housewife of color. But instead of challenging the stereotypes, Gabrielle revels in them, just like Charo and Shakira before her.

Yet for all these stereotypical portrayals of people of color, the subject of racism never enters the picture. Well, that's not quite true. Bree revealed her true (white) colors this season when she caught Matthew Applewhite in Danielle's bedroom. She exclaims with disapproval, "Danielle, is there a *black man* under your bed?!" Yet racism is a daily reality for people of color.

Andrea, who pastors an affluent Lutheran church in New Jersey, deals with the double bind of being black *and* female.

She's been mistaken for the church cook, a housekeeper, and a maintenance worker. "Once, I walked into a meeting at a seminary, and no one would talk to me. They assumed I was there to clean up!" During seminary, one of my classmates, an African American man who grew up in an affluent section of Atlanta, was stopped more than twenty times while driving in town. Someone asked him what the problem was, and he said, "I was DWB—driving while black." And recently, during the coverage of Hurricane Katrina, it was noted that when people of color were shown carrying goods out of flooded stores, they were identified as "looters." But when white residents were caught in similar circumstances, they were "searching for essentials."

These anecdotal accounts speak to a pervasive and serious problem—the way systemic racism shapes and distorts our culture, securing power for the majority at the expense of the minority. In truth, *Desperate Housewives* is simply telling the story our society has written, but in vivid color.

If race and racism are cavalierly misused on *Desperate Housewives,* then poverty is abused outright. There are no poor people on *Desperate Housewives,* because being poor is bad. When Gabrielle and Carlos lose their money, they go to extreme lengths to disguise their temporary poverty, fearing their friends will think less of them. When Bree and Rex cover up Andrew's hit-and-run accident, they dispose of the evidence by leaving the car unlocked in a bad part of town. Waiting for something to happen, Rex says to Bree, "How can you be sure this will work?" "Because," says Bree, "I have faith in the poor." The attitude of the residents of Wisteria Lane is summed up in an exchange between Carlos and Gabrielle. Carlos, who wants to donate his car to charity in a fit of altruism, says, "Buying more stuff isn't going to make us happy." Gabrielle snaps back, "That's just a lie we tell poor people to keep them from rioting!" This line is meant to reveal how shallow Gabrielle really is, but she's still the sympathetic character.

For those who aren't able bodied, Wisteria Lane is a nightmare of porch steps and uncut curbs. There was an episode about

Lynette befriending a deaf woman whose husband openly mocks her ("It's not like she can hear me!"). But it was used to comic effect. Lynette's meddling leads the husband to leave his deaf wife, and she angrily confronts Lynette. The scene ends with the woman signing, "bitch!" and storming out of the room.

Then there is poor Caleb Applewhite, who has been given the nonspecific diagnosis of "slow." He spends the first few episodes chained in the basement. (You know those mentally handicapped people—they can be so violent.) Rather than letting her son fall into the evil judicial system or, worse yet, foster care, Betty keeps him under lock and key, controlled through a series of verbal and physical threats.

If your particular concerns lie beyond issues of race, poverty, and disability, *Desperate Housewives* tosses a few other social problems into the mix. Lynette got hooked on drugs, just like Dierdra, Zach's birth mother; Gabrielle was physically abused by Carlos; and this season, Bree is quickly becoming an alcoholic. Unfortunately, the writers of *Desperate Housewives* ascribe to the Scarlett O'Hara school of social work, either fixing the issue with a single act or saying "Fiddle dee dee! I'll think about that tomorrow!"

Yes, *Desperate Housewives* is pretty clumsy when it comes to racism, poverty, and other social issues. But there is one minority group that is portrayed with honesty and grace—homosexuals. One small plot involves John's hunky roommate, who tries to blackmail Gabrielle into sleeping with him so he can prove to himself he's not gay. As he desperately explains to Gabrielle why he's so anxious to have sex with a woman, his words of confession have the ring of truth. Another plot involves Andrew Van De Kamp, who may or may not be gay, but is definitely a rotten person. When Andrew "comes out" to his parents, Bree is horrified. She speaks for everyone who doesn't accept homosexuality when she pleads with Rex, "We need to put him in Christian counseling so it doesn't become a lifestyle!"

The heart and soul of *Desperate Housewives,* the show's creator and head writer, Marc Cherry, is gay, so it's no wonder that he is able to breathe life into these particular plot lines. He has a feel for both sides of the conversation because he's been there, done that. In an interview featured on the first season DVD, Cherry admits that some of the dialogue used in Andrew's coming out scene was taken verbatim from his own life. Trying to reassure Andrew that she's OK with his confession, Bree tells him, "Andrew, I would love you even if you were a murderer!" In fact, those were the first words Mrs. Cherry said to son Marc when he came out to his family.

The nice thing about the way *Desperate Housewives* deals with homosexuality is that it fosters engagement in the issue, presenting a variety of sides in more or less sympathetic light. The show doesn't spend much time on the problems faced by homosexuals in our society, but it also doesn't downplay those problems or reinforce harmful stereotypes. I only wish the writers had a similarly sympathetic approach to other minority groups because it would make it much easier for a Christian to enjoy the show.

Wisteria Lane is a wonderful place to be, a place of beauty and perfection where the sun is always shining and the children are always well mannered (except for Lynette's). Of course, once you start paying attention, pulling the background into the foreground, you start to see who's missing for this suburban Eden, and it can be disquieting. But for those of us who call ourselves Christian, it's more than disquieting—it's downright unfaithful.

Part of what it means to be a Christian is to imitate Jesus—to try to conform ourselves to his image. It's an impossible task, and we shall all fall short of the glory of God, but that's the life to which we are called. A Christian life is not one of grand gestures or heroic moments (although it can be on occasion), but one of daily formation. Each morning, we try to live *like* Christ and live *for* Christ. In our struggle to be like Christ, it turns out there is wisdom in the trite question, "What would Jesus do?" If we take this question seriously, it can change the way we do everything—even the mundane, everyday tasks. For example, I have a friend who has decided to drive like a baptized person, which has radically altered how he approaches traffic. Instead of road rage, he now has road grace.

So if we are supposed to be like Jesus and value what he values, then what's missing on Wisteria Lane should cause us great concern. Jesus spent his life with the poor and the oppressed. He ate with despised tax collectors; he defended prostitutes; he touched lepers; he cared for the poor. Everything he did was in keeping with his mission statement, proclaimed before the synagogue in Nazareth through the reading from Isaiah:

> "The Spirit of the Lord is upon me,
>   because he has anointed me
>   to bring good news to the poor.
> He has sent me to proclaim release to the captives
>   and recovery of sight to the blind,
>   to let the oppressed go free,
> to proclaim the year of the Lord's favor." (Lk. 4:18–19)

If this is what Jesus came to do and what Christians are called to do in his name, we'll have to find someplace other than Wisteria Lane to do it. As entertaining as the trials and triumphs of the housewives can be, we should never forget who did not get invited to this party. Look around, and you may have a sudden realization; "Captain! Where are the Christians?"

CHAPTER 9

The Gospel According to Mary Alice

I once preached a five-minute sermon (stop the presses!) that asked the congregation this question: "If someone defined what it means to be Christian just by observing your life, what would the faith look like?" I'm told this was a popular sermon (probably because it was so short), but at the time, what I saw was a sanctuary full of squirming people. Even for a pastor, it's a sobering thought. What does Christianity look like in my life?

Well if that's a sobering thought, consider for a moment what Christianity looks like on *Desperate Housewives*. In this dark comedy nothing is sacred and everything in life is potential fuel for the fire. It doesn't matter whether it's motherhood, marriage, friendship, or sex—every topic is mined for its comedic potential. This is especially true when it comes to Christianity.

Desperate Housewives serves up a version of Christianity that is based on liberal stereotypes and tired assumptions. Christians are portrayed as ineffectual, judgmental hypocrites. If anyone identifies as a Christian, you can be sure there is something funny about to happen. Don't believe me? Who is the first person we meet on Wisteria who calls herself a Christian? Mrs. Huber, who was helping sort through the charred rubble of Edie's home. Explaining why she was letting Edie move in with her, Mrs. Huber says, "It's the only Christian thing to do." In the next moment, Mrs. Huber discovers that Susan was the one who caused the fire, and she uses this information to blackmail her. (Oh those crazy Christians!) This prejudiced portrayal of Christianity drives me nuts, because it's difficult enough calling yourself a Christian without the most popular show on television serving up a warped definition of the faith.

My trouble is compounded because I'm a pastor. When people learn what I do, they either seek spiritual counseling from me or treat me like I'm some sheltered invalid who's not used to the shocks of the outside world. Walk into a party and get introduced as "Rev. So and So," and suddenly the best jokes are going untold and you've been shuffled off to a corner with a glass of white zinfandel. Being identified as a pastor, or as a Christian, is hard because people make assumptions based on their own stereotypes and negative experiences with Christians.

Of course, there is no such thing as a "typical Christian." When you say you are Christian, do you mean like Anne Lamott or Pat Robertson? Are you more Joyce Meyer or Thomas Merton? Do you read Jim Wallis or Joel Osteen? There's no one way of being Christian, and anyone who tells you otherwise is selling something. Sure, there may be only one body of Christ, but there are many gifts, which is why the portrayal of Christians on *Desperate Housewives* is so appalling. So let's take a closer look and see what faith looks like on Wisteria Lane.

Here's the scene. Gabrielle wants to hire a hotshot lawyer to get Carlos out of jail. But the lawyer, David, has fallen in love with Gabrielle and won't take the case. Gabrielle offers to have an affair with David, but she won't leave Carlos. "I'm Catholic," she explains. "Divorce is not an option." "But you'll have an affair?" David asks incredulously. Gabrielle gives him a look and says, "I said I was Catholic, not a fanatic!"

Jesus was pretty hard on the Pharisees, who were the defenders of the religious *status quo*. In Matthew, he says to the people, "The scribes and the Pharisees sit on Moses' seat; therefore, do whatever they teach you and follow it; but do not do as they do, for they do not practice what they teach" (Mt. 23:2–3). In other words, the Pharisees said one thing and did another. Just like Gabrielle, they were hypocrites, clinging to the letter of the law but ignoring the intent.

The Christians on *Desperate Housewives* are more like the Pharisees than they are like Jesus. Sister Mary Bernard (whom Gabrielle calls Sister Mary Hot Pants) talks about caring for the poor and visiting the prisoners, but she's got her eye on Carlos. Why else would she offer him a pamphlet entitled "The Catholic Guide to Annulment?" (For the *true Desperate Housewives* fans, I hope I'm not spoiling anything, but I think it's pretty clear Sister Mary will be back from Alaska and out of the habit, as it were. You could tell by the way she wore high heels to scrub the altar steps. This nun thing is cramping her style.) And of course there is Bree, who reads the Bible, goes to church, and is guilty of manslaughter and aiding and abetting. On *Desperate Housewives*, Christians say one thing and do another.

You hear this same charge leveled against Christians in the press. Not a few conservative Christian leaders have denounced *Desperate Housewives* for being morally corrupt. Yet when these pronouncements are covered in the press, it's generally noted that the show is extremely popular in the traditionally conservative markets, such as Atlanta and Salt Lake City. Whether it's said or not, the suggestion is the same—Christians are hypocrites.

Another popular myth that *Desperate Housewives* exploits for humorous ends is that Christians are ineffective, especially the clergy. Father Crowley, the Catholic priest, keeps trying to counsel Gabrielle, but she simply uses him. Sitting at Mama Solis's bedside, Gabrielle questions Father Crowley about forgiveness and repentance, since she knows he's aware of her affair with John. Although he tries to draw the line with her, he's incapable of getting through. Finally she asks, "If I wait, does my repenting still count?" He sighs and says yes. So much for priestly authority.

Another ineffective Christian is the prison chaplain, shown leading a couple's therapy session. The nondescript clergyman tries to lead the group, asking in his blandest counseling voice, "How does that make you feel?" But no one is listening to him, and at the end of the scene, it looks as if a fight is about to break out.

But the funniest and therefore least effective Christian leader is the good Rev. Sykes, who is brought in by Bree to "cure" Andrew's homosexuality. This is the old "pastor as ultimate weapon" cliché, where a family at wits' end finally calls in the big religious guns to discipline the wayward child. Rev. Sykes is all deference and piety, the kind of person who *would like* to be shuffled off to a corner with a glass of white zinfandel. He starts by spewing the Christian line about choosing homosexuality, the inevitable guilt, and the need for repentance. "All you need is a little faith and a desire to change!" But when Andrew says he has nothing to repent for because he's pretty happy just the way he is, Rev. Sykes has nothing more to say. Of course, Bree has plenty more to say and ends up revealing Rex's taste for S&M. At the end of the scene, only a stunned Rev. Sykes and an amused Andrew remain at the table, and Andrew says, "We should do this more often." The message is clear; in the face of real issues, Christians have nothing to offer. It's all pie in the sky in the sweet by and by.

According to *Desperate Housewives,* Christians are hypocrites and ineffective—or at least out of touch with real life—which makes them suckers. In other words, Christians are naïve and easily fooled. When Gabrielle wants to get rid of Sister Mary Bernard, she simply lies, telling Father Crowley that Sister Mary is sleeping with Carlos, and Father Crowley is foolish enough to believe her. When Andrew meets with Rev. Sykes to discuss his "homosexual cure," Andrew instead reveals his twisted plan to destroy his mother. This happens, of course, after Rev. Sykes has promised (on the Bible) not to reveal anything about their conversation. (This is a particularly poorly done scene because Protestant pastors don't operate this way.)

I don't know what Bible the writers of *Desperate Housewives* are reading (here I'm showing my own naiveté, suggesting that they are reading the Bible) but they clearly don't understand Jesus' words to the disciples as he sends them out. "See, I am sending you out like sheep into the midst of wolves; so be wise as serpents and innocent as doves." (Mt. 10:16) Christians aren't suckers; we just know what game is really being played.

However, one Christian stereotype on *Desperate Housewives* has more truth to it than I'd like to admit—Christians are judgmental. When Paul Young asks Mrs. Huber why she black-mailed Mary Alice, Mrs. Huber says, "It's better to take money from a bad person than a good one." "She wasn't bad!" cries Paul. "Read your Bible, Paul. Suicide's a big no-no." These are some of the last words Mrs. Huber says before Paul clocks her with a blender. Her bitter judgment of his beloved wife pushes him over the edge into a murderous rage. (Let *that* be a lesson to you!)

Bree is similarly judgmental, but with less violent results. Sitting on the couch with Andrew, looking at his baby photos, she tells him a tender story of his birth, how he almost died, and how she told the doctors to ignore her and save little Andrew. Then Bree looks him deep in the eyes and says, "Andrew, if you don't change who you are, you won't go to heaven." (Let *that* be a lesson to you!)

I wish I could counter this stereotype with any integrity, but I can't. Plenty of Christians in American society are quick to judge others, and too often they have their own TV shows. Lately Pat Robertson has been leading the pack. He proclaimed that Hurricane Katrina was God's judgment on the immorality of New Orleans. (One should note that the hurricane's surge missed the French Quarter, so either God has some affection for us sinners or suffers from bad aim.) After the November elections, Robertson condemned the people of Dover, Pennsylvania, for voting the pro-creationism school board members out of office, warning them not to bother asking God for help because they had voted God out of their city. (His words sounded rather like a radical imam declaring a *fatwa*.) And the latest news from Robertson? The tragic stroke suffered by Israeli Prime Minister Ariel Sharon was God's way of punishing him for giving the Gaza Strip back to the Palestinians. Robertson is several bubbles off plumb, but he still couches his judgments in Christian terms.

What does Robertson think Jesus is talking about in Luke's gospel?

> Be merciful, just as your Father is merciful. Do not judge, and you will not be judged; do not condemn, and you will not be condemned. Forgive, and you will be forgiven; give, and it will be given to you. A good measure, pressed down, shaken together, running over, will be put into your lap; for the measure you give will be the measure you get back. (Lk. 6:36–38)

Christians are called to be humble, not to raise themselves to the position of God. We have no basis on which to render judgment of another person. We can only witness to the truth of Jesus Christ as we understand it and live lives that are a testament to what Christ can do in us and through us. If more Christians embodied this sort of humility, *Desperate Housewives* wouldn't have so much material to work with.

Ineffective, gullible, judgmental, and hypocritical—the Christian faith according to *Desperate Housewives* is a sorry excuse for a religion. If Christianity really looked like this, I'd be the first one out the door. Luckily, this is not an accurate depiction of the faith or the faithful.

On the other hand, it does accurately capture a movement within our culture that distrusts organized religion. I regularly encounter people like this, who like what Jesus has to say, but think there is nothing of value in the church. "I'm spiritual but not religious," they tell me. (My friend Lillian once quipped, "That's like saying you love Jesus, but hate all his friends.") This is precisely how the writers of *Desperate Housewives* approach faith. They're hard on organized religion, but big on vague spirituality.

There's not a lot of practicing of faith on Wisteria Lane. You never see the housewives pray or engage in any devotional practices. They don't even celebrate any religious holidays. You'll never find a tacky crèche set cluttering Susan's house; you'll never see an Easter basket left for the Scavo boys. Even Gabrielle, who practices yoga, doesn't approach it as a spiritual discipline. As my friend Rooth noted, "It's shopping, not yoga, that gives her a sense of inner peace."

Bree Van De Kamp does attend church and own a Bible, and she has a pastor to call in times of trouble. The opening montage of episode fifteen tells us, "Bree Van De Kamp believed in old-fashioned values: respect for God, the importance of family, and the love of country." But watch carefully, and you'll notice that Bree uses religion the same way Edie uses push-up bras—just a prop to give the right appearance. She clings to the faith when it supports her particular point of view, but conveniently ignores it when it thwarts her desires. For example, before Bree and Rex decide to hide Andrew's hit-and-run accident, Bree is shown reading the Bible. Mary Alice's voice interprets the scene, "Bree knew it was wrong, but like most sinners, she would think about that tomorrow." In other words, despite her public persona as an upstanding Christian, Bree doesn't let scripture interfere with *real* life. As I once heard William Sloane Coffin say, "She uses scripture as a drunk uses a lamp post—for support, not illumination."

In all fairness, I should note that Gabrielle is also a Christian. But again, her Roman Catholic faith is nothing more than a prop, used to generate funny situations rather than as an expression of her inner character. During the second season, when she needed to talk to Father Crowley, she went to confession. Father Crowley opened the door and asked, "How long has it been since your last confession?" Gabrielle sneered, "Who cares?" (Cue laugh track.)

Yet for all the jokes *Desperate Housewives* makes about religion, it is an oddly spiritual show. Mary Alice is not just the source of the initial drama, she's the benevolent presence that guides us through the twists and turns of Wisteria Lane. Mary Alice sees everything from her vantage point in the afterlife, which makes heaven appear to be nothing more than balcony seating. She is the all-seeing, ever-sympathetic spirit that interprets life.

Watching the show, I was struck by the way the action is framed by Mary Alice's voice-over and the words she uses. After the usual recap, every episode begins with the narrator making some general statement about the characters and their situations. "Bree Van De Kamp believed in old-fashioned values." "Gabrielle Solis knew all men were the same." Sometimes Mary Alice's remarks are connected directly to the action, but more often than not, they are tangential in nature. At the end of the show, Mary Alice returns to her earlier theme, interpreting what we've just seen, as the camera shows us brief shots of the women.

What's remarkable is that Mary Alice's final commentary is usually laden with spiritual language. She speaks of guilt and forgiveness, sinners and saints, light and darkness, angels and demons, love and compassion. From her heavenly vantage point, Mary Alice seems to see all the messy human interactions on Wisteria Lane through a theological veil. What's more, she makes some remarkable theological statements, some of which are quite profound.

At the end of the episode in which Carlos has had a conversion experience and Bree has allowed George to die, the soothing voice of Mary Alice speaks about the true nature of humanity: "Sinners can surprise you. Compassion and cruelty can live side by side in one heart. And anyone is capable of anything." It's like reading a hipper version of Luther's catechism, on the true sinful nature of man. Last season, in the episode in which we learn that Mrs. McCluskey lost her only child, and Bree agrees to engage in a little kinky sex with Rex, Mary Alice speaks about the nature of true love. "Love sustains us through trying times. And long after we're gone, love remains." Sounds more than a little like Paul: "(Love) bears all things, believes all things, hopes all things, endures all things. Love never ends." (1 Cor. 13:7–8a)

Whether the writers intend to or not, *Desperate Housewives* even has its own operating theology—and not all of it is good. When Gabrielle discovers she is pregnant, she goes to see Father Crowley. "God is screwing with me!" cries a distraught Gabrielle. Father Crowley's response makes my theological head spin. "Have you done something that would warrant being punished?" This one-for-one exchange sort of theology is bad news, but Gabrielle doesn't question it.

There's also an odd understanding of forgiveness on the show. Bree sits in judgment of George as he lies dying from a drug overdose. "I want to help you, but I can't until I forgive you, George. You need to admit what you've done." George doesn't confess, so Bree doesn't forgive—nor does she call 911 for help. The message? Don't confess and you die!

Compare that episode to a recent one in which Tom Scavo is offered a job at Lynette's firm. Lynette doesn't think he can do the job, but Tom really wants it. And Lynette still feels guilty about having cost Tom his promotion at his previous firm. In a poignant scene, Lynette says, "I'll let you take this job on one condition. I need you to forgive me for costing you your promotion." Tom looks at her and smiles, "I already forgave you." The message? If someone really loves you, then forgiveness is fore-given, which is closer to my own understanding of Christian forgiveness.

I could go on and on, because if you start to pay attention to the implied spiritual and theological messages of *Desperate Housewives,* you could write a different book, albeit a strange and warped text full of half-truths and outright heresy. The point I'm trying to make is this: *Desperate Housewives* deals with spiritual issues not by accident, but on purpose. Why? Because human beings are spiritual beings, and, like it or not, we hunger for meaning and connection that transcend simple bodily experience.

This fact of human life is precisely why we have organized religion. We need a way to make sense of our spiritual experiences. We need a community that holds us accountable and gives us a sense we are not alone. We need the practices and habits of religious life that connect us to our spiritual selves and to God, the ground and goal of our being.[1] Our spiritual nature creates a desire to set off on a journey; religion provides the roadmap. Without it, we wander the land, making nonsense instead of sense.

Desperate Housewives wants to have it both ways. The show indulges in the current cultural bias against organized religion while simultaneously lifting up the profoundly spiritual nature of human life. In other words, explicitly and implicitly, *Desperate Housewives* is asking the big questions, but has no hope of ever finding any answers.

CHAPTER 10

Judgment Day—or Barbie Does No Damage?

"So what's the verdict?" This was Nell's question to me. "Is *Desperate Housewives* OK or should it be avoided at all costs?" I hesitated to answer. After all, I'd sort of developed a fondness for the show. "I think it's pretty harmless," I replied. "Oh," said Nell, "so you're going with the 'Barbie does no damage' theory."

It's a helpful theory. When my daughter was born, I announced to my friends that (1) I would never dress her in pink and (2) I would never allow her to have a Barbie, those plastic talismans of patriarchy. You can guess the rest of the story. As it turns out, my daughter's favorite color is purple, but pink is a close second, so her closet is full of pink clothes, just as her toy chest is full of Barbies. I could sit and lament my fall from feminist perfection, but instead, I've decided to go with the theory that Barbie does no damage. Whatever messages Barbie and her 52–18–32 measurements convey, I am more than able to counteract them. But is the same true for *Desperate Housewives?*

I guess it depends on who you are, on your perspective and values. If you're a mom who has decided to stay home with young children, but who wonders over the third load of laundry if you have made the right decision, the gorgeous exteriors and nonstop excitement of the housewives might deepen your doubts. If you're a man fretting over a stalled career, growing soft in the middle, and fearful of the next wave of corporate downsizing, the steady parade of desirable hunks marching confidently down Wisteria Lane might make you wonder if you've lost the capacity to measure up. If you're a middle-aged woman in a marriage grown tired, the high drama and constant sexual fireworks of *Desperate Housewives* might be the final straw that drives you toward despair. If you're a feminist, the show's exaggerated depiction of feminine beauty and obsession with gaining male approval might mar an otherwise lively night of thoughtless entertainment. If you're African American, you might find the scarcity of people of color deeply troubling.

From a Christian perspective, any number of facets of the show should give one pause. There is plenty to object to in *Desperate Housewives,* much to complain about, and something to offend almost everyone, especially, perhaps, people of faith. But, let's admit it; the show is basically likeable and often fun to watch. What, then, is the answer to Nell's question? Is *Desperate Housewives* OK, or should it be avoided? One good way to answer this question is to say that it is simply a matter of balance and awareness. Watching *Desperate Housewives* is like having a taste for chocolate. We all know it's not really good for us, no matter what scientists discover about its health benefits. But that doesn't mean you can't eat it. It simply means you can't eat a lot of it, and you need to make sure the rest of your diet is balanced. A little chocolate and a lot of broccoli is not a bad way to live.

Translating this into Christian terms, nothing is fundamentally wrong with watching *Desperate Housewives* as long as we know what we're taking in, and as long as it's not the *only thing* we're taking in. Jesus once said, "There is nothing outside a person that by going in can defile, but the things that come out are what defile" (Mk. 7:15). I don't know what the spiritual equivalent of broccoli is, but there is plenty of solid and nourishing spiritual fare out there. In addition to scripture, there are programs and books that do far more to nourish the soul than does *Desperate Housewives.* Tune into *Now* with Bill Moyers or listen to *Speaking of Faith* with Krista Tippett. Try reading books by Anne Lamott, Kathleen Norris, or Leif Enger. You could even put a little John Calvin on your plate (I'm pretty sure *The Institutes* counts as broccoli), and you might develop a taste for sturdier Christian fare. Here's the bottom line: if your faith is in good shape and well nourished, then a *little Desperate Housewives* won't do you much harm.

Indeed, we can even imagine using episodes of *Desperate Housewives* to teach Christian lessons, even if only as a source of negative examples. I asked my niece Madeline, who is a hardcore fan, if she could think of any lessons she's learned by watching the show. She paused and then said, "Well, I've learned that even though Gabrielle is pretty, she's not very nice. I guess buying stuff doesn't make you a good person." Madeline shows that a well-told tale of failure is still instructive.

I've also used *Desperate Housewives* in adult education with good success. While most of the show is late night soap opera entertainment best enjoyed in the confines of your own home, a couple of episodes are worth studying in the context of a faith community. For example, episode eight, entitled "Guilty," starts and ends with images of blood and water. Gabrielle asks Father Crowley about forgiveness and salvation. Lynette hits bottom with her drug addiction. Mrs. Huber meets her untimely demise. Susan and Mike talk about the nature of trust. There are lots of images and issues for Christians to explore. When my adult education class screened this episode, some of the questions we asked were: What is the importance of the human body in the Christian faith? How often do you see images of blood and water during the course of the show, and what do they mean? What does this show teach us about repentance? The truth is that if we put on our theological lenses, popular culture has a lot to offer.

Yet beyond the issue of balance and the possibility that a few episodes might offer something of substance, we should think about how a television show such as *Desperate Housewives* affects our emotional life. Zella, who works for a church, was explaining why she loves the show. "It makes me laugh! There have been times I've wanted to whack my husband with a plate—something heavy, like Pfaltzgraff—but I didn't. It's sort of fun to watch someone actually do it!" What Zella is experiencing is catharsis.

Catharsis is a sort of emotional release, an experience that cleanses the soul. First defined by the Greek philosopher Aristotle, catharsis was what audiences were supposed to feel after watching a tragic play. A cathartic experience is one that allows you to feel emotions without going through the experience that causes them. We may feel murderous, but if we watch someone act out a murder and see the inevitable consequences, we are able to release those feelings. In other words, catharsis is a sort of emotional detox, clearing out all the dark and dangerous desires.

I suspect Zella is not alone. I'll bet there are many people who find *Desperate Housewives* cathartic. My friend Jennifer told me the reason she started watching the show was because she was so mad at her husband, Chris. "He was gone almost every weekend hunting, and I was just furious. I guess I liked watching a show where the women were just as mad at their husbands as I was." But midway through the season, Jennifer realized that the show wasn't helping her. Instead of helping her get over her anger, it was fueling her rage, helping her nurture her grudge against Chris. She describes her realization in Christian language. "I was convicted by the Spirit for watching that show, and I had to stop." For Jennifer, *Desperate Housewives* was not cathartic. Instead, it was mimetic.

Mimesis, source of the words *mimic* and *mime*, means to imitate. The Greek philosopher Plato explored the power of mimesis, especially as it related to poetry. The chief worry was that if people imitated what they saw on stage, they should only be exposed to ideas and stories that ennoble and build character. This was the beginning of censorship.

The idea of mimesis is behind many of the battles in the culture war. If people imitate what they see in our culture, the culture must be held to a higher standard. No more of these tawdry plots. No more of these tank tops. If we're going to become a better society, pop culture needs to lead the way.

Unfortunately, it's not as simple as that. Each person brings a unique way of seeing the world and gathering information based on his or her own experiences, values, habits, and ways of perceiving. What is instructive to one is destructive to another. In other words, one person's mimesis is another person's catharsis. In light of this, censorship in the name of building a better society seems like a fool's enterprise.

We're right back where we started, aren't we? No closer to having some final word on the value of *Desperate Housewives*. Is it cathartic? Or is it mimetic? Does it allow us to control our baser instincts? Or does it encourage us to wallow in our own self-centeredness? The world may never know.

In fact, asking questions such as these gives *Desperate Housewives* a dignity and gravitas it doesn't merit. Let's be serious. *Desperate Housewives* is innocuous, just a bit of fluffy entertainment aimed at drawing in as many viewers as possible. And to that end, it is wildly successful. It aims no higher, has no nobler purpose, than to generate advertising revenue for ABC. Twenty years from now, only trivia buffs will be able to tell you who Bree, Susan, Lynette, and Gabrielle were (the same folks who can name all of the sons on *Bonanza* or who know the meaning of "master of your domain" on *Seinfeld*). As for *Desperate Housewives,* the psalmist has it right: "The wind passes over it and it is gone" (Ps. 103:16).

Ironically, recognizing that *Desperate Housewives* is nothing more than flotsam drifting by at this moment in the cultural stream may bring us even closer to answering the question of value. Now we arrive at the truth. *Desperate Housewives* is successful at this moment in our cultural history because it is exactly what the advertisers want it to be—a highly polished surface in which we see the reflection of our deepest and darkest hopes and desires. That is what captures and holds our attention for an hour every week. Troubled by what you see on *Desperate Housewives?* Look closer. We have met the enemy, and she is us. If we don't like what we see on Wisteria Lane, maybe it's time to pull ourselves away from the television and take a look in the mirror.

Putting this in Christian terms, on the surface *Desperate Housewives*" is a light and lively bit of entertainment, but look beneath the surface and you'll find a stammering attempt to name all the places we are broken and lost. At the conclusion of season one, Mary Alice offers her own interpretation. She looks at the other women, "each in her own way so brave, so determined, and so very desperate." Considering the plight of each housewife in turn, she concludes: Lynette—"Desperate to venture out, but afraid of what she'll miss." Gabrielle—"Desperate to get what she wants, even when she's not exactly sure of what that is." Bree—"Desperate for life to be perfect again, even though she realizes it never really was." Susan—"Desperate for a better future if she can find a way to escape her past."

I like Mary Alice's list of problems, but I think she's too close to her subjects to see things clearly. If we step back from Wisteria Lane for a moment, far enough back so that the characters are reduced to their barest outlines, we can see things a little differently. There is something universal about these women. Their struggles are our struggles; their flaws are our flaws, the flaws of every woman, of every man. At the dramatic heart of these four characters lie the great struggles, the great failings, the great temptations that we face every day.

First, there is the issue of control. One theologian described sin as the attempt to control the things we're not supposed to control and the refusal to control the things we are supposed to control. Bree isn't just about perfection, but about the desire for misplaced control. In a post 9/11 world, where our own government tells us that something terrible could happen at any time, there is a growing desire for this same sort of control. It shows in the way we overschedule our children, obsessively read self-help books, allow our civil rights to erode, and even cling to religious leaders who assure us that if we get right with the Lord, we are assured of the good life, right now. Like Bree polishing the silver, we're fighting the chaos of modern life one day planner at a time. All would be well, we tell ourselves, if only we could get organized and get some control.

Second, there is the problem of the restless, unsatisfied heart. Augustine once prayed, "For Thou madest us for Thyself, and our heart is restless, until it repose in Thee."[1] Gabrielle represents our restless, desperate search for contentment. Asked why she married Carlos in the first place, she tells John, "I thought he'd give me everything I ever wanted." "Didn't he?" asks John. "Yes, but it turns out I wanted the wrong things." Everything Gabrielle does—from shopping to sex to flirting—is part of a losing battle to achieve some sort of peace. She knows something is missing. But no matter what she buys or whom she sleeps with or how much money she has, she cannot find it. Is there any doubt that our society suffers from the same longing? When was the last time you heard someone say they needed a little "retail therapy"? Something is missing, and we know it, and until we find it, we'll just keep filling the emptiness with stuff.

Then there is the temptation to deny our true identity, forgetting that we are beloved children of God, made in the image of God. Mary Alice gets Lynette all wrong. Lynette isn't about the struggle between independence and motherhood. No, she represents our desire to figure out our real identity in the tension between work and self, between the outer life and the inner life, between what we do and who we are. Like so many women and men, Lynette struggles to care for her family and achieve some professional success. But it goes much deeper than that. What Lynette is seeking is a sense of identity, an assurance that at the end of the day, she has worth. She didn't find it in the home, so now she's looking at work.

Finally, there is the problem of failed love and broken relationships. Mary Alice may think Susan wants a future, but what Susan really wants is love. She wants to be loved and to love someone in return. This yearning for acceptance, this search for true intimacy is at the heart of every person, no matter who they are or where they are. We long to find the other, the one who completes us. Of all the women's plights, this one is the most desperate.

Now don't think for a moment that naming and facing these issues are evidence of weakness. Christians know that honestly owning up to the truth about our broken lives is not an act of cowardice, but a sign of bravery. Mary Alice, in her own way, recognizes this. At the end of her final monologue in season one, she says, "I not only watch, I cheer them on, these amazing women. I hope so much they'll find what they're looking for." Having said this, though, Mary Alice yields to discouragement and hopelessness. "But I know not all of them will," she says. "Sadly, that's just not the way life works. Not everyone gets a happy ending." She might as well have said, "Tune in next year to see whose life falls apart!"

This dark conclusion to the show is no accident. In describing his vision for *Desperate Housewives,* Marc Cherry said that he wanted to explore what's really behind the American dream. On the surface, Wisteria Lane looks perfect, exactly what every American aspires to. But lurking in the verge and behind the doors are the dark secrets and troubling realities of life. Cherry often refers to this as "the dark stuff." We may think everything is wonderful, but he's on a quest to prove that everyone is corrupt, no matter how good and successful and perfect they appear to be on the surface, and that every person is capable of good. At the end of the day, though, the darkness wins. "Not everyone gets a happy ending."

Desperate Housewives has done a great job of spinning society's stereotypes, prejudices, and anxieties into gold. You've got to hand it to the writers; they know exactly who we are and where we're at, which is why twenty-five million people tune in week after week. The problem is the writers seem to have no idea how we got there nor where we go from here.

Cherry is right about one thing. There is darkness, but not the darkness of hidden murders or adulterous affairs. The real darkness, out of which all other darkness flows, isn't found on the outside, but within. And there's a name for it—sin.

On the surface, then, *Desperate Housewives* is a frivolous comedy, but at its deepest level—from a Christian perspective— it's a profound tragedy. There is honest, if accidental, confession of sin, but no true forgiveness. There is a hunger for a "happy ending," but no genuine hope. There is a cry of the heart, but no answer. There is a sense of being lost, but no one to find us. There is peril, but no savior.

We don't like to talk about sin and salvation much in our culture. Sin is such a downer, such an embarrassment. Talk of sin makes us feel guilty and unworthy. Talk of salvation challenges our need to be autonomous and self-reliant. We even tend to avoid such talk in church. Too much talk about sin and salvation causes people to leave the congregation and find a happier, more uplifting way to be spiritual, usually with a cup of coffee and the *New York Times* crossword. At the end of the day, though, what is at the heart of all our desperate struggling is sin. At a basic level, we are broken people, incapable of making ultimate meaning or sense of our lives. Until we come to terms with this fundamental truth, we will always be desperate.

Thank God there is an answer. It comes to us through the grace of God, in the person of Jesus Christ. Jesus came to release the captives—even those living on Wisteria Lane—from the bondage of sin. Jesus understands the grasping for control in the Brees of the world, the restless hearts, the denial of sacred identity, and the failed relationships of the Gabrielles, the Lynettes, and Susans who make up the human race. Jesus not only understands; Jesus comes to rescue us. Once we encounter the love of Christ, nothing is the same. Wherever there is honest confession of sin, in Christ there is true forgiveness. Wherever there is a cry of the heart, Christ answers in compassion. Whenever someone is lost, Jesus the Good Shepherd goes out searching until the lost is found. Whenever someone is in peril, Jesus comes to save. Suddenly we have inner resources we never imagined, possibilities we never dreamed of. The struggles of daily life—for control, for meaning, for peace, for love—are gathered up into the love and acceptance of God. No longer plagued by questions, we have the only answer we'll ever need. We are children of the living God, who loves us and calls us into the world not to be desperate, but to be like Christ, and bring the light into a world of darkness.

I leave you with the words of John.

> In the beginning was the Word, and the Word was with God, and the Word was God. He was in the beginning with God. All things came into being through him, and without him not one thing came into being. What has come into being in him was life, and the life was the light of all people. The light shines in the darkness, and the darkness did not overcome it. (Jn. 1.1–5)

Marc Cherry and the housewives might call this a happy ending. I call it the gospel of Jesus Christ.

APPENDIX

Study Guide

(Note: If you have access to the first season DVDs of Desperate Housewives, I have recommended which episode is most appropriate for each chapter.)

Chapter 1: Who Do You Say That I Am?
(Recommended viewing: Pilot Episode)

The entire design of the mega-hit *Desperate Housewives*—from the characters to the costumes to the setting to the soundtrack—is meant to create a particular mood: the perfect life. The four main characters represent certain advertising demographics. The backdrop against which these characters perform is hypersensual and hyper-sexualized.

1. If you had to locate Wisteria Lane (and the city of Fairview), where would it be?
2. Which of the four main characters do you find sympathetic? Which of the four do you find unsympathetic (or just plain old pathetic)? Why?
3. When you think of heaven, what does it look like? Are there any "heavenly" aspects to Wisteria Lane? Do you think this is accidental?
4. Why do you think this show is so popular? Why do women watch it? Why do men watch it?

Bonus Fan Question: After watching the pilot episode, do you see any clues about the main characters and their relationship to the basic mystery?

Chapter 2: Is Zero Even a Size?

(Recommended viewing: Episode 9)

Desperate Housewives has a specific understanding of female beauty: thin, young, and sexy. The Christian tradition isn't preoccupied with beauty, but with faith. How do real women, who come in a variety of shapes and sizes, understand where true beauty comes from?

1. Name someone famous who is considered beautiful. What about this person sets her or him apart from everyone else?
2. How does popular culture shape and influence your definition of beauty?
3. Read Proverbs 31:10–31 (the virtuous woman). Based on this passage, what are the desirable characteristics of a woman? Why do you think these characteristics were desirable?
4. Read Song of Solomon 7. What do you think this woman looks like? Is she beautiful?
5. Name someone you know whom you would define as a beautiful person. What characteristics does this person have that makes him or her beautiful?

Bonus Fan Question: Who is the fairest of them all? Why?

Chapter 3: For Better, for Worse…and for Now
(Recommended viewing: Episode 13)

Desperate Housewives features a variety of dysfunctional marriages. Lynette and Tom struggle with children and careers; Bree's quest for perfection drives Rex away; Gabrielle and Carlos's marriage is marked by violence and infidelity. Yet for all the craziness, these couples deal with some of the real issues in marriage—children, intimacy, fidelity, trust—but in a less than realistic way. The biblical version of marriage isn't much more realistic. Perhaps the best way to approach marriage—and love—is by understanding that we are loved by God and called to love one another in a way that is selfless, not selfish.

1. Describe the perfect marriage. What are the most important aspects of marriage? Whom do you think of when you think of a good marriage?
2. What, in your experience, are the sources of stress in marriage?
3. Read Ephesians 5:21–33 (or 1 Cor. 14:34–35, Col. 3:12–25). What is the Pauline understanding of marriage? How are the husband and wife supposed to relate to each other? Is this a realistic description of marriage?
4. What is the purpose of marriage?
5. Read 1 Corinthians 13. How does this description of love fit with your own experience? How does it differ? If you substitute the word *God* for *love* do you come to a different understanding of the passage?

Bonus Fan Question: Name the most realistic marriage moment on *Desperate Housewives*.

Chapter 4: Children—The Perfect Accessory
(Recommended viewing: Episode 18)

Parenting on *Desperate Housewives* is a hobby more than a calling. The mothers of Wisteria Lane are little more than broad caricatures of socially constructed stereotypes. Bree is the perfect mother; Lynette is the stay-at-home mother; Susan is the best-friend mother. In real life, parenting is not a part-time occupation, but a full-time occupation, one that demands creativity, love, discipline, and patience.

1. As a parent—or as someone who has watched other people parent—who do you think does a good job of parenting on *Desperate Housewives*?
2. What is the greatest challenge these days for parents?
3. Choose one of the following passages and discuss what kind of parenting the passage describes. Are these biblical parents true to life? (Gen. 27; 2 Sam. 18; Judg. 11:29–40; Mt. 15:21–28; Lk. 8:40–56)
4. What are the "big moments" *(kairos)* in parenting in your opinion? Can you recall any of these big moments with your own parents?
5. What are the "little moments" *(chronos)* in parenting? Can you recall any of these little moments with your own parents?

Bonus Fan Question: Who is the best parent on Wisteria Lane?

Chapter 5: Working Girls

(Recommended viewing: Episode 14)

As with most television shows, it's difficult to tell what the women of Wisteria Lane do for money. No one is shown juggling a career with home life except for Lynette. But this is a part of life most women and men know all too well. Careers and work play an exceptionally important part in our modern lives, which is not good news. Any striving for identity—at home or at the office—that doesn't include God is a recipe for dissatisfaction.

1. What is the difference between a job and a career?
2. What is the purpose of work in your life? Does it bring you satisfaction?
3. For working parents—what are the challenges you face? What one change would improve your life? Where are you making compromises?
4. For at-home parents—what are the challenges you face? What one change would improve your life? Where are you making compromises?
5. Read John 10:10. What do you think Jesus means by "abundant life"? What would an abundant life look like for you?
6. Read Exodus 20:8–11. What is the connection between work and Sabbath (rest)? How do you keep the Sabbath holy?

Bonus Fan Question: Who has the most unrealistic job on *Desperate Housewives?*

Chapter 6: Sex and the Suburbs—or Dance of the Seven Tank Tops

(Recommended viewing: Episode 9)

Sex is everywhere on *Desperate Housewives,* and most of it is illicit. One strange message on the show is that mothers aren't sexy. There is also very little realistic sex; it's all sizzle and no steak. This reflects our culture's general discomfort with sexuality but fascination with sex. Christians need to come to terms with their own understanding of human sexuality and what it means to be creatures of flesh and spirit.

1. Who is having good sex on *Desperate Housewives?* Who is having not-so-good sex on the show? How important is sex on this show?
2. How realistic is this in your own experience? (Don't over share!)
3. Is American culture obsessed with sex? How can you tell?
4. What is the difference between "sexy" and "sensual"?
5. Read Genesis 1:26–31. What is the message about sex inherent in this passage? Is sexuality a gift or a curse?
6. How does Jesus, the word made flesh, change your understanding of the word body?

Bonus Fan Question: Which housewife has a realistic sex life?

Chapter 7: With Friends Like These...

(Recommended viewing: Episode 16)

Female friendship is the underlying premise of *Desperate Housewives*. Despite all the drama and mystery, Bree, Lynette, Susan, and Gabrielle stick together. Most women have a strong circle of friends who play an important role in their lives, people who offer support, wisdom, laughter, and comfort. One of the challenges to female friendships is competition. But in the end, friendship is of higher value. Jesus himself called his disciples "friends."

1. What role do friends play in your life? How do you express, explore, and strengthen your friendships?
2. Name a time when a friend (or friends) made a big difference in your life. Was there anything holy about this moment?
3. Is there such a thing as female competition for masculine approval? Can you give an example of it? How do you cope with it?
4. Read the book of Ruth. Why does Ruth follow Naomi? How do these two women embody the values of friendship?
5. Read John 15:12–15. What is the difference between being called a servant and being called a friend? Why is friendship more important?
6. How would the world change—how would your life change—if we could all be friends as Jesus describes?

Bonus Fan Question: Which housewife would you like for a friend and why?

Chapter 8: As You Have Done to the Least of These
(Recommended viewing: Episode 17)

The foreground of *Desperate Housewives* is a comedy drama about perfect women living not-so-perfect lives. The background is a stylized version of the perfect world. But lots of people are missing or misrepresented: people of color, the poor, people with disabilities. Although the housewives don't mix with these groups much, Jesus certainly did. And in real life, we deal with racism and prejudice of many kinds.

1. Why do you think a "typical place" such as Wisteria Lane pays so little attention to people out of the mainstream?
2. Name a piece of popular culture that features people out of the mainstream. How are these people portrayed? Is it fair?
3. As you reflecting on your own life, how does *Desperate Housewives* differ from the real world as you know it?
4. Read Luke 4:18–19. Jesus speaks of the poor, the captives, the blind, and the oppressed. Who are these people in our culture?
5. How do you—or could you—participate in Jesus' mission, as described in Luke?

Bonus Fan Question: How can you tell that Gabrielle Solis is Hispanic?

Chapter 9: The Gospel According to Mary Alice
(Recommended viewing: Episode 19)

Even though a majority of Americans identify themselves as Christian, talk of spirituality on *Desperate Housewives* does not mention Jesus. The show reinforces old stereotypes about Christians—that they are judgmental, ineffective hypocrites. Yet although the show is not supportive of religion, it is very spiritual, engaging in its own brand of theology. In the end, "*Desperate Housewives* asks big spiritual questions it simply can't answer.

1. Do you ever hesitate to identify yourself as a Christian? Why or why not?
2. What stereotypes do people have about what it means to be Christian? Are these stereotypes based in reality? Where do they come from?
3. Read Matthew 10:5–26. What does Jesus say disciples are supposed to do? How does this translate into your life?
4. What are the basic requirements to call oneself a Christian?
5. Who are the public Christians who represent your particular kind of faith?

Bonus Fan Question: Setting aside labels, who on Wisteria Lane *acts* as a Christian would act?

Chapter 10: Judgment Day—or Barbie Does No Damage?
(Recommended viewing: Final Episode of First Season)

Desperate Housewives is a pretty harmless piece of entertainment, even though it includes plenty that one could find objectionable. But it doesn't take too many risks as it tries to appeal to a wide audience. As Jesus says, "There is nothing outside a person that by going in can defile, but the things that come out are what defile." (Mk. 7:15) The problem is not with *Desperate Housewives,* but with our culture in general. In the end, the show reveals some universal human flaws (dare I say sins?), but doesn't offer any hope. That hope is found in Jesus Christ.

1. How do you keep your faith strong? What works for you? What could you change that would help you strengthen your faith?
2. Name something from popular culture (movies, books, TV shows) that you think make a positive contribution to your faith, even if the contribution is only a negative example.
3. Think about the difference between catharsis (something that provides emotional release) and mimesis (something that causes you to imitate what you see.) Is *Desperate Housewives* cathartic or mimetic?
4. Do you think darkness lurks behind every door—as it does on Wisteria Lane? How do Christians respond to this?
5. Consider the four struggles represented on the show: the struggle for control, the problem of the restless heart, the denial of our sacred identity as children of God, and the struggle to form and maintain an intimate relationship. Which of these struggles resonates with you? How does your faith help you cope with this struggle?

Bonus Fan Question: Memorize Mark 7:15 so that you have an answer for anyone who says "Christians can't watch *Desperate Housewives.*"

Notes

Chapter 1: Who Do You Say That I Am?

[1]Gary Levin, "Housewives Lifts ABC's Spirits—and Ratings," USA Today, 4 October 2004, at: http://www .usatoday.com/life/television/news/2004–10–04–desperate-wives-abc-comeback_x.htm

[2]Lynn Elber, "ABC Seeks 'Housewives' Viewers at Cleaners," ABC.com, January 2, 2006, at: http://abcnews.go.com/Entertainment/wireStory?id=980419&CMP=OTC-RSSFeeds0312

[3]"Prime-Time Nielsen Ratings," Associated Press, Forbes.com, December 7, 2005, at: http://www.forbes.com/feeds/ap/2005/12/07/ap2374681.html

[4]"Housewives Ends Year on Stable Ratings Note," December 5, 2005, at: http://www.getdesperate.com/news/051205_01.shtml

[5]Kevin Downey, "NBC's Latest Woe: Flight of Affluent," Media Life Research, November 3, 2005, at: http://medialifemagazine.com/artman/publish/article_1065.asp.

[6]Maria Elena Fernández, "Men love their 'Housewives'," Los Angeles Times, Nov. 12, 2004, at: http://www.azcentral.com/ent/tv/articles/1113housewives.html

[7]"Parents TV Council Spurns Fox Shows, 'Housewives'," Associated Press, October 19, 2005.

[8]"Desperate Savior: Marc Cherry Turns Domestic Angst into a Network's Hope," B&C Beat, 9/20/2004, http://www.broadcastingcable.com/article/CA454227.html?verticalid=311&industry=Top+of+the+Week&industryid=1024.

Chapter 2: Is Zero Even a Size?

[1]From Mame, book by Jerome Lawrence and Robert E. Lee, 1958.

Chapter 3: For Better, for Worse... and for Now

[1]"Christians are more likely to experience divorce than are non-Christians," Barna Research Group, December 21, 1999, available online at: http://www.barna.org/FlexPage.aspx?Page=BarnaUpdate&BarnaUpdateID=170.

Chapter 4: Children— the Perfect Accessory

[1]This brilliant theological insight came from my friend Shannon Craigo-Snell.

Chapter 5: Working Girls

[1]"Women in the Labor Force: A Data Book," U.S. Department of Labor, Bureau of Labor Statistics, 2005, at: www.bls.gov/cps/wlf-databook-2005.pdf

[2]Louise Story, "Mother Yale", New York Times, 20 September , 2005, section A, page 1, col. 7.

[3]"Money (That's What I Want)," words by Berry Gordy and Janie Bradford, ©1959, 1962 Jobete Music Incorporated.

[4]Judith Warner, NewYorkTimes.Com blog, "Are You In, or Out?" January 16, 2006.

[5]Ibid.

Chapter 8: As You Have Done to the Least of These

[1] The U.S. Department of Justice gave the following statistical breakdown of the prison population nationally: 43.6 percent of prisoners are white, 39.2 percent black, 15.4 percent

Hispanic, other ethnic groups 1.8 percent. Paige M. Harrison and Jennifer C. Karberg, "Prison and Jail Inmates at Midyear 2003," *Bureau of Justice Statistics Bulletin* (May 2004): 8, available online at http://www.ojp.usdoj.gov/bjs/pub/pdf/pjim03.pdf.

Chapter 9: The Gospel According to Mary Alice

[1] I borrowed this phrase from the theologian Paul Tillich.

Chapter 10: Judgment Day—or Barbie Does No Damage?

[1] Augustine, *Confessions,* trans. E.B. Pusey (Whitefish, Mont.: Kessinger Publishing, 1942), book 1, section 1, page 1.